Will Dogs Chase Cats in Heaven?

Will Dogs Chase Cats in Heaven?

PEOPLE, PETS, AND WILD ANIMALS IN THE AFTERLIFE

Dan Story

Kingdom Come Publications

Also by Dan Story

Defending Your Faith, Kregel Publications
Christianity on the Offense, Kregel Publications
Engaging the Closed Minded, Kregel Publications
The Christian Combat Manual, AMG Publishers
Where Wild Things Live, Naturegraph Publishers
Should Christians Be Environmentalists?, Kregel Publications
Plus fifteen apologetic booklets, Joy Publishing

To my much-loved wife and best friend, Lisa.
I introduced her to the wild creatures that share our planet.
She showed me how to love them more.

Contents

Introduction

Dog Lessons for People
Enjoy the simple pleasure of a walk
Run and play daily
Be loyal, faithful, and quick to forgive
Always drink plenty of water
Sometimes it is best to sit close and listen
Follow your instincts
Keep digging until you find what you want
Avoid biting when a growl will do
Accept all of life's treats with gratitude
Love unconditionally
(ANONYMOUS)

A few years ago one of my best friends died. His name was Sam, and he lived fifteen carefree, happy years. I never had a more trustworthy friend: faithful under any circumstance, sensitive to my every mood, eager to please regardless of inconvenience, my protector. He was the embodiment of patience, commitment, and unconditional love. Sam was a true friend—and I loved him.

You're right. Sam is a dog. A coal-black Labrador Retriever with beautiful, intelligent, expressive golden eyes. I named him after the "rough-looking mongrel dog" in Louis L'amour's first novel, *Hondo*. Sam was every bit as dedicated and bright as the canine companion of my cowboy hero.

During the last few years of Sam's life, I watched this powerful 85-pounder slowly succumbed, with dignity and without a whimper, to old age. His pure black coat whitened across his muzzle and around his eyes and paws. His tight, hard muscles vanished, replaced by protruding hip and shoulder bones and numerous bulbous lipomas (benign fatty tumors common in old dogs). His eyes were clouded with cataracts, and he could barely hear. One shin was perpetually swollen, and although the vet determined it was probably cancer, Sam was too old for surgery. He struggled to get up and down and walked with a stumbling gait, sometimes losing his balance. During the last year of his life, he never let me out of his sight. If I went into my study, he followed me. If I sat down to read in the living room, he lay at my feet. Anywhere I went in the house, even for a minute or two, he struggled painfully to his feet and followed me. Sam wanted to spend all of his few remaining months in *this* life in my presence.

It's my heartfelt belief that I will see Sam again in Heaven—and I know I'm not alone in believing this. According to an ABC poll, forty-seven percent of pet owners believe that after death they will be reunited with their beloved pets in Heaven.[1] Numerous Christian scholars agree. They acknowledge the likelihood—if not outright certainty—that earth-bound animals alive today will inhabit Heaven. Christian apologist C. S. Lewis, philosophy professor Peter Kreeft, well-known authority on Heaven, Randy Alcorn, and the president of the Christian Research Institute, Hank Hanegraaff—to name a few—have all expressed belief that animals may well inhabit Heaven. I'll share some of their thoughts in a later chapter.

Actually, Sam's death was not the first time I became interested in the eternal fate of non-human life. The first time was on my 20th wedding anniversary. My wife and I were in Moab, Utah, exploring Arches National Park. When we called home that evening to check on our kids, who were in college and high school at the time, they told us our Golden Retriever, Bear, had died. We were grief stricken and felt terrible that we were not home to comfort him (and our kids) as he was dying. To make matters worse, our fifteen year old son was left with the sad task of burying his dog "brother." In our motel room that night, I tearfully wrote a eulogy for Bear to preserve the memory of his life. I wondered at the time if he would be there to greet my wife and me in Heaven?

Theologically, this question raises two issues. The less controversial is whether or not animals will inhabit the redeemed and restored new heaven and earth[2] prophesized by Isaiah, Ezekiel, Hosea, Peter, John, and others. The Bible makes it abundantly clear they will—and there is ample biblical evidence to support this. We'll examine many of these passages later.

The more thorny issue is whether or not the non-human inhabitants of this *New Earth* will include pets, domesticated animals, and wild creatures that presently dwell on *this* Earth. In other words, when Jesus returns at the end of this present age to set up His eternal Kingdom and populate it with redeemed, resurrected humans, will earth-bound animals be part of the redeemed and resurrected?

This is a provocative and, admittedly, baffling question—one even Solomon, the wisest man who ever lived, apparently pondered: "Who knows if the spirit of man rises upward and if the spirit of animals goes down into the earth?" (Eccl. 3:21). Perhaps animals wonder the same thing. In a 1989 cartoon in the Sunday paper, the late Charles Schultz let us in on a conversation between Lucy and Snoopy. Lucy is reviewing something Snoopy had written:

Lucy: "I don't think your subject is serious enough. You should write something that is really thought-provoking.

Write about something that has been a puzzle since the world began."

Snoopy's new title: "Are There Dogs in Heaven?"[3]

Of course, polls and cartoons do not determine truth. The ultimate answer to the question of animal immorality is what the Bible reveals. In the following chapters, I will present as much biblical evidences as I can muster to support my belief that animals alive on Earth today will dwell in the eschatological *Peaceable Kingdom* described in Isaiah chapter eleven and elsewhere.

I realize this is a controversial topic and that a necessary degree of speculation is required. The Bible simply doesn't explicitly reveal the ultimate destiny of animals that die *before* Jesus returns to establish the redeemed new heaven and earth (Rom. 8:19-23). Nevertheless, I believe by carefully and systematically analyzing relevant passages in Scripture, as well as other evidences we'll examine, a compelling case can be made that at least sentient non-humans (animals able to perceive and feel things) *will* continue to exist after physical death in the future new heaven and earth, along with redeemed humanity. Moreover, I'll demonstrate that arguments against the immortality of non-human life are merely assumptions without legitimate biblical support. As C. S. Lewis put it, rejecting animal immortality because we lack full understanding of "God's method in the revelation" is an argument from silence, which, Lewis pointed out, is "very weak."[4]

In order to develop my thesis, we'll explore a variety of related topics, such as: What is God's perspective on non-human life? Do they have value to Him independent of humans, or did He create animals solely for people to use, enjoy, and consume? What do animals think, feel, and experience? (You may be surprised what recent studies in animal behavior have revealed!) What is there about sentient animals that would lead us to conclude that they, like humans, have immaterial minds distinct from their physical brains—and thus have souls? (I'll demonstrate that recent studies in brain science support this conclusion.) Did God give animal souls immortality? If so, will animals be resurrected?

Now, let me add this: Some readers will disagree with my conclusions. Fair enough. But *nothing* I suggest in this book is outside biblical possibilities or contrary to established, orthodox biblical truths.

And, finally, please understand this: I am not elevating animals to human status, either on Earth today or the age to come. Only humans were created in God's image (Gen. 1:26-27), and we are far more valuable to God than non-human life (Matt. 6:26; 10:31; 12:11-12). Nor am I attempting to impart more intrinsic worth on animals than what God Himself does. This will become clear in the first chapter. Finally, what I conclude in this study is *not* out of character of the love, compassion, grace, and creativity of "our great God and Savior, Jesus Christ" (Titus 2:13).

CHAPTER 1

Do Animals Have Value to God Independent of Their Value to Humans?

All things bright and beautiful
All creatures great and small,
All things wise and wonderful,
The Lord God made them all.
CECIL FRANCES ALEXANDER, 1848

I once asked my wife what she thought God had in mind when He instructed Adam to name all the animals (Gen. 2:19-20). She replied, "It shows that God values the animals He created, and Adam was given the responsibility to care for them." Lisa was right, of course. And in her case she took God's directive to name the animals personally.

In 1979 my family and I moved to a small, rural community in the foothills of Southern California. We brought with us our delightfully funny Golden Retriever, Bear, a paranoid former stray cat appropriately named Wild Kitty, and two orphaned, adolescent raccoons that Lisa was raising as a volunteer at a wildlife rescue center. Their names were Frik and Frak, and we would release them into the wilds when they were old enough to survive on their own. We also inherited two goats that came with the property—which my daughter (who was reading *Gone with the Wind* at the time) named Rhett and Scarlett.

This was just the beginning. In no time at all, my wife surrounded herself with a menagerie of other animals. And yes, she named them all. Besides Bear and Wild Kitty, Frik and Frak, Rhett and Scarlett, our property became home to Wolf (a German Shepherd); Charger (another stray cat); Sallyanne, Poppy, Sunflower, and Starflower (more goats); Radish (a rooster); Bess, Pepper, Skuzzy, Scraggy, Buffy, Orphy, Omelet, and Kate 1, 2, and 3 (hens); Toady (a toad, naturally); and Lizzie the lizard. Had they hung around, I'm sure every bird in our trees or opossum that scouted our vegetable garden or coyote that howled in the night would also have been given a name!

Now I have to admit, my kids and I enthusiastically supported my wife and enjoyed our "mini farm," with all its various critters. We even got used to drinking goat's milk!

Unfortunately, when you surround yourselves with so many animals, sooner or later they begin to die. The most heartbreaking was our Golden Retriever, Bear. He was officially my wife's dog but became a beloved pet for our entire family—and hands down the favorite of all our animals. I was a fairly new Christian when he died, and, as I mention in the introduction, his death was the first time I can remember pondering whether or not pets will be in Heaven.

More than thirty years have come and gone, and I'm more convinced than ever that my family and I will one day be reunited with Bear and Sam, and all the other animals we have loved and lost, in the future new heaven and earth (Rev. 21:1). I also believe that this prophesized *Peaceable Kingdom* will be the eternal home of all sentient wild and domesticated animals (e.g. Isa. 11:6-9).

There are several reasons I believe this, and each chapter in this book will explore one of them. In this chapter, I'll lay the foundation for the rest of the book by establishing that animals are of tremendous value to God—*independent* of the human race.

Why Did God Create So Many Animals?

A few years ago I heard the host of a well-known nationally broad-cast talk radio program make this statement: "There is no reason for animals to exist unless people exist." There is no doubt that God had the human race in mind when He created Earth (Ps.115:16), and in this sense animals probably wouldn't exist if humans didn't. Even so, the pundit's comment was misleading because it implies that animals are of little value to God, and put on Earth solely to benefit people. As this chapter will show, however, such an assump-tion does not reflect God's love and concern for non-human life. God created much of the earth to be a home for wild animals—creatures that offer no particular benefit to humanity.

Nevertheless, the pundit's remark does raise a valid question. Did God create all the animals that inhabit the planet solely for human use and pleasure? To put it differently, if animals have no purpose except to serve people, why did God create so many varieties that have absolutely no instrumental value for humans? Indeed, why would God create millions of species of animals but only be concerned about the human race?

To answer these questions, we must begin with the Bible's earli-est comments on the relationship between humans and animals. According to the biblical narrative, God created animals and the first humans on the same "day." (*Yom* in Hebrew is translated a literal day as well as an indefinite period of time). Afterwards, He placed Adam in the Garden of Eden to "work it and take care of it" (Gen. 2:15). Because it was "not good for the man to be alone," God brought "all the beasts of the field and all the birds of the air" for Adam to name and to be his "helper" (18-19). We're not told how long, but for a spell animals were Adam's only companions. God knew all along, however, that animals would not be a "suitable helper" for Adam, so God created Eve (20b-22).

At this point in early human history, assuming the Genesis narrative is in chronological order, animals continued to be Adam and Eve's only companions until they were banished from the Garden of Eden and had children (3:23-4:2). In fact humans and animals probably continued to enjoy peaceful relationships for many generations beyond Adam and Eve. There is no biblical record of antagonism between humans and wild animals in the first eight chapters of Genesis. It wasn't until after the worldwide Flood, which occurred during Noah's generation, that animals began to fear humans—and humans began to eat animals (Gen. 9:2-3).

There are two significant things revealed in this account. First, God's *intended* relationship between people and animals was one of companionship and peaceful co-existence. Second, animals were not only companions they were also "helpers."

God intended for some animals to become domesticated and serve the human race: "Abel kept flocks," Genesis 4:2 tells us, probably to provide wool for clothing and milk for food.

Domestication reached new heights when wild canines (recent scientific studies suggest wolves) became more than helpers, when they became our friends. This initiated a remarkably new relationship between humans and animals; dogs were the first of an amazing menagerie of creatures that over the centuries would become our pets: cats, horses, hamsters, rats, monkeys, rabbits, parakeets, parrots, fish, turtles, lizards, snakes, and even insects (think ant "farms") have been welcomed into our homes (I'm sure many readers can add to this list).

But the Genesis account doesn't explain why God created so many different "kinds" of animals (and plants) that are of *no* benefit to humanity—some of which would eventually become a nuisance and even dangerous to the human race. Domesticated animals represent only a tiny fraction of the total number of creatures that inhabit Earth. Tens of thousands of incredibly amazing and wonderfully diverse animal species have been scientifically named, and it's estimated there may be as many as *eight million* more animals and plants yet to be discovered.[1] Considering these statistics, it seems evident that God had other purposes in mind than just serving humanity when He created so many varieties of animals. I believe He also created them for His own good pleasure, His own enjoyment (e.g. Ps.104:31).

The Bible clearly teaches that God loves, finds joy in, and carefully provides for the survival and welfare of non-human life—*independent* of His even greater love, joy in, and provision for human life (36:6). Let's look at the biblical evidence for this.

"The earth is the Lord's and everything in it"

This statement in Psalm 24:1 is key to understanding the relationship God intended between humans and the rest of creation. People do not own the earth. God does—and everything else He created. This is plainly stated in other passages in the Bible. Centuries before David penned Psalm 24, Moses wrote in Deuteronomy, "To the LORD your God belong the heavens, even the highest heavens, the earth and everything in it" (10:14). Everything means everything, and everything includes animals. In fact God specifically emphasized his ownership of the animal kingdom: "Every animal of the forest is mine, and the cattle on a thousand hills. I know every bird in the mountains, and the creatures of the field are mine" (Ps. 50:10-11). Our side of this relationship is to be God's caretakers over *all* creation, including animal life (Ps. 8:6-8). As I've established elsewhere, this directive was given to Adam and passed on to all future generations throughout the entire Earth.[2]

The Bible mentions dozens of animals by name, and even in antiquity biblical characters recognized their inherent value. King Solomon "taught about animals and birds, reptiles and fish" (1 Kin. 4:33). Job told his accusers that people can learn from fish, birds, and other animals (Job 12:7-8; cf. Prov. 6:6; 30:25). Furthermore, God often used animals for His own purposes. When He instructed the prophet Elijah to go into hiding, He used ravens to bring him food (1 Kin. 17:1-6). God used a great fish to save Jonah's life (Jon. 1:17) and a small fish to provide the money for Jesus and Peter to pay the temple tax (Matt.17:24-27). In the account of Balaam and his donkey, it was the donkey—not Balaam—that saw the angel sent to prevent Balaam from doing evil (Num. 22). Jesus used the sparrow and raven as illustrations in spiritual lessons (Luke 12: 6-7, 24). Notice Jesus chose birds people generally considered insignificant (the sparrow) or devious (the raven). Perhaps most remarkable of all, wild animals accompanied Jesus during His temptation in the wilderness (Mark 1:13). We'll examine this passage in a later chapter.

God Desires All Animals to Fulfill the Purpose of Their Creation

There are numerous passages in the Bible, especially in the Old Testament, that describe how God ensured the survival and propagation of animal life. It begins as early as Genesis chapter one (also see Ps. 36:6; 104:10-21; 145:9,15; 147:7-9).

The creation story relates that God designed Earth from the beginning to support animal life. Before the first creatures were spoken into existence, He created vegetation to produce "plants bearing seed according to their kinds and trees bearing fruit with seed in it according to their kinds" (Gen. 1:12). Thus, food and shelter were available when animal life began to inhabit Earth (Gen. 1:30). After their creation, God charged the sea life, the birds of the air, and land dwelling "livestock, creatures that move along the ground, and wild animals" to multiply and fill the seas and cover the earth (Gen. 1:20–25).

Prior to creating Eve, God instructed Adam to name the animals (Gen. 2:19). By assigning him this duty, God showed a personal attentiveness for *individual* species of animals—not just the broad categories of created "kinds." This also suggests that Adam was given a stewardship role in the animal kingdom. As Baylor University Professor Susan Bratton points out, Adam's instructions to name the animals "did not imply the power of life and death over [animals] . . . but rather sets them in relationship to humankind."[3] This relationship was to be one of stewardship, and it continues today. When people name their pets and zookeepers name the wild animals under their care, they are accepting responsibility for their welfare. Visitors to zoos also relate better with animals that have names.

Nowhere is God's providential care for animals portrayed more dramatically and personally than His protection of wild and domesticated animals during the sin-cleansing, worldwide Flood. God made sure that a genetic stock of every kind of animal was preserved on Noah's ark to later repopulate the earth (Gen. 6:19-7:3). This command was not qualified. It included what many people consider "vermin" as well as animals that would eventually become dangerous predators. God did not save just the animals that were profitable to people.

After the floodwaters receded and the wild animals were released to repopulate the earth (Gen. 8:17-18), God made a covenant with the human race that included *all* animal life. It was an unconditional, permanent covenant, and it continued to reveal God's providential care for animals:

Then God said to Noah and to his sons with him: "I now establish my covenant with you and with your descendants after you and with every living creature that was with you—the birds, the livestock, and all the wild animals, all those that came out of the ark with you—every living creature on earth. I establish my covenant with you: Never again will all life be cut off by the waters of a flood; never again will there be a flood to destroy the earth" (Gen. 9:8–11).

This same concern for the welfare of non-human life continued with the emerging Jewish nation. God commanded the Israelites to adhere to specific stewardship guidelines that included provisions for *wild* animals. In the Sabbath year instructions, for example, God told the Israelites:

For six years you are to sow your fields and harvest the crops, but during the seventh year let the land lie unplowed and unused. Then the poor among your people may get food from it, and *the wild animals may eat what they leave.* Do the same with your vineyard and your olive grove (Ex. 23:10–11, emphasis added; also Lev. 25:1–7).

Additionally, Moses told the Israelites prior to their conquest of the Promised Land, "If you come across a bird's nest beside the road, either in a tree or on the ground, and the mother is sitting on the young or on the eggs, do not take the mother with the young. You may take the young, but be sure to let the mother go" (Deut. 22:6-7). Had these instructions to preserve breeding populations of animals harvested for human consumption been followed throughout human history, there would be fewer endangered species today.

God Also Made Provisions for Domesticated Animals
God has equal concern for the humane treatment of domesticated animals—animals He allows the human race to use for food and

labor. Unlike wild animals, people are directly responsible for the health and nutritional needs of domesticated animals. This is clearly expressed in Proverbs 12:10, "A righteous man cares for the needs of his animal," and in God's instructions on the care of farm animals (e.g. Deut. 22:1-4). There are other passages in Scripture that express God's desire—and often with explicit instructions—for the humane treatment of domesticated animals.

Centuries before the Mosaic Laws set forth instructions for the care of domesticated stock, the patriarch Jacob recognized his responsibility to care for nursing sheep and cows (Gen. 33:13). Later, Moses directed the Israelites to work only six days so that on the seventh day they and their oxen and donkeys may rest (Ex. 23:12). He instructed them not to "muzzle an ox while it is treading out the grain," apparently so it may feed on what drops to the ground (Deut. 25:4).[4] God's command to protect domesticated animals also includes an *enemy's* livestock (Ex. 23:4–5). Even the Ten Commandments have a provision to care for domesticated animals: "Six days you shall labor and do all your work, but the seventh day is a Sabbath to the LORD your God. On it you shall not do any work, neither you, nor your son or daughter, nor your manservant or maidservant, *nor your animals*" (Ex. 20:9–11, emphasis added).

Although these instructions were to benefit the Israelites, the fact that God commanded farmers to provide food and humane treatment for their livestock shows that even animals the human race are allowed to use for labor and food are valuable to God.

Animals Have Value to God *Independent* of People

Nowhere does the Bible communicate God's love and joy for animals independent of His love and joy for people more clearly than in Job 38 and 39 (the longest passage in the Bible that focuses on non-human creation) and Psalm 104 (the most descriptive passage of God preparing nature to support animal life). These passages mention specific animals and specific habitats that God prepared for individual varieties of animals. The wild donkey was given "the wasteland as a home, the salt flats as his habitat" (Job 39:6). The Ostrich "lays her eggs on the ground and lets them warm in the sand" (13-14). The eagle builds "his nest on high" and "dwells on a cliff . . . a rocky crag is his stronghold" (27-28). God "makes springs pour water into the ravines; it flows between the mountains" to give "water to all the beasts of the field." There "the wild donkeys quench their thirst" (Ps.104:10-11). God waters the trees He created, and there "the birds make their nests; the stork has its home in the pine trees. The high mountains belong to the wild goats; the crags are a refuge for the coneys" (17-18). God "provides food for the raven" (Job 38:41) and the lions "seek their food from God" (Ps.104:21). Indeed, all animals, the Psalmist declares, look to God "to give them their food at the proper time" (27). The oceans as well as the land are included when the Psalmist passionately praises God for all He has made:

> How many are your works, O Lord!
> In wisdom you have made them all;
> the earth is full of your creatures.
> There is the sea, vast and spacious,
> teeming with creatures beyond number,
> living things both large and small (24-25).

There are two significant things we can learn from these passages. First, God provides food, shelter, and habitats for wild animals *apart* from human considerations. Second, only God is present and observes much of what happens in nature. In many of His reflections on wild nature, humans are totally absent. God causes rain to "water a land where no man lives, a desert with no one in it" (Job 38:26). He asked Job, "Do you know when the mountain goats give birth? Do you watch when the doe bears her fawn? Do you count the months till they bear? Do you know the time they give birth?" (39:1-2). The self-evident answer to these rhetorical questions is that *only God* observes these events and is present when they occur.

In sum, God breathes His "Spirit" into animals to give them life (Psalm 104:30). He establishes their territories, provides their shelter, and gives them their daily food (also see Job 38:41; Ps.136:25; 145:15-16; 147:8-9; Joel 1:19-20; 2:21-22; Luke 12:24). God didn't create animals and then relinquish total authority over them to the human race so that people can use and abuse them as they please. Animals have intrinsic worth because God created, values, and finds joy in them (Ps.104:31; Col. 1:16).

Animals Respond to God

In response to God's love and provision, through beautiful poetic language, all creation—including wild animals—is portrayed worshiping and praising the Creator. Psalm 148 speaks of angels and other "heavenly hosts" praising God alongside "sea creatures" and "wild animals and all cattle, small creatures and flying birds" (148:7, 10). Speaking through the prophet Isaiah, God says, "The animals of the field will honor me, jackals and ostriches, because I provide water in the wilderness, and rivers in the desert" (Isa. 43:20). The last verse in the last Psalm concludes: "Let everything that has breath praise the LORD" (Ps.150:6; also Ps. 65:12–13; 96:11–12; 98:4–8). At the end of this present age, explains the book of Revelation, "every creature in heaven and on earth and under the earth and on the sea, and all that is in them [will sing] 'To him who sits on the throne and to the Lamb be praised and honor and glory and power, for ever and ever'" (5:13).

That animals praise and worship the Creator further confirms their value to God independent of humanity. As Professor Bratton put it, "We have to reject the notion that wild nature is only valuable if it is useful to humans. If wild nature praises God, that alone justifies its existence."[5] We'll explore the topic of animals praising God more fully in a later chapter. The point for now, as theologian Richard Bauckham points out, is this: "If we gave more attention to the creatures as our fellow-worshippers, we would not be so prone to instrumentalize them, to regard them as having value only if we can make use of them for our needs and desires."[6] In short, animals are important to God apart from the human race.

Jesus and Animals

One of the common criticisms hurled at Christianity by radical animal rights advocates is that the Bible is indifferent to the welfare of animals (which we've already seen is clearly untrue). In particular, critics claim that Jesus showed little concern for animal life. Well known animal rights advocate Peter Singer is an example. He writes, "The New Testament is completely lacking in any injunction against cruelty to animals, or any recommendations to consider their interests. Jesus himself showed indifference to the fate of nonhumans when he induced two thousand swine to hurl themselves into the sea."[7]

Singer's allegation is not justified by the text. It was not Jesus but the demons that drove the pigs into the sea (see Matt. 8:30–32). Allowing this to happen is not the same as condoning it. To claim otherwise is to read meaning into the passage that flies in the face of the actual narrative—as well as the whole Scriptural teachings on Jesus and non-human life.

But more important, for Jesus to have shown indifference to non-human life would have been *impossible*! As the second member of the triune Godhead, Jesus could not be apathetic toward wild and domesticated animals because God is passionately concerned for their welfare and survival. In other words, as the incarnate Son of God, Jesus would have shared the Father's love and concern for all animal life, wild and domesticated.

The primary purpose of Jesus' incarnation was to open the door for humans to become reconciled to God through His sacrificial death on the cross for our sins. His Second Advent will include the removal of nature's curse (Rom. 8:20-32; Rev. 22:3; cf. Gen. 3:17-19); the establishment of a new heaven and earth (Isa. 65:17; Rev. 21:1); and the redemption of *all* creation alongside His people—which of course will include animal life (Rom. 8:19-23— more on this later). Nevertheless, even when Jesus walked this Earth He still demonstrated an appreciation and concern for animals. He told His disciples that not a single sparrow "is forgotten by God" (Luke 12:6). He pointed out that God provides animals their food (Matt. 6:26; Luke 12:24) and is concerned for their welfare (Luke 12:6). Indeed, it was Jesus who abolished animal sacrifices. And this raises one more issue that needs to be addressed before moving on.

Aren't Animal Sacrifices Inhumane?

I suspect some readers may be wondering about the apparent inconsistency between God's love for animals and His instructions in Leviticus and elsewhere to include animal sacrifices in religious activities. This is a fair concern, so let me make a couple of observations.

Animal sacrifices were never pleasing to God in the sense of His desired response from sinful hearts. After King David committed adultery with Bathsheba, he cried out to God for forgiveness and wrote, "You do not delight in sacrifice, or I would bring it; you do not take pleasure in burnt offerings. The sacrifices of God are a broken spirit; a broken and contrite heart, O God, you will not despise" (Ps. 51:16-17; cf. 40:6-8).

On the other hand, animal sacrifices—the shedding of innocent blood—vividly depict the gravity of sin and the heartbreaking
cost of redemption. In God's revelatory plan for human salvation,
animal sacrifices in the Old Testament point directly to the ultimate, once-and-for-all sacrifice of Jesus Christ on behalf of rebel-
lious sinners (see Heb. 10:1-14). I can see no more powerful or
effective way for God to illustrate this crucial message. But animal
sacrifices do not lessen God's love for animals and should not dis-
tract us from this fact. Moreover, slaughtering animals for sacrificial purposes was done quickly and humanely; it was no different
than butchering animals for human consumption today. In fact
much of the edible portions of sacrificial animals were used for
food (see Deut.12:27; 16:5-7; 18:3). And remember, it was Jesus
who ended the need for sacrificing animals (Heb.10:3-14). Many
believe this was illustrated when He drove the money changers
and sacrificial animals out of the temple court (John 2:14-16).

* * *

Let me summarize this chapter, which lays the theological foundation for the rest of the book. God created all animal life. They are
His possessions. He enjoys them and desires that they live and pros-
per, and He has created specific habitats and foods to ensure this
will happen. A few varieties of animals serve humanity as domestic
stock and companions, but the vast majority was created to live
wild and free. As the prophet Isaiah observes, God "fashioned and
made the earth, he founded it; he did not create it to be empty,
but formed it to be inhabited" (45:18). In short, animals are both
dependent upon and loved by God. Therefore, it's irrefutable that
they are of tremendous value to Him.

Standing alone, the data in this chapter does not translate into
explicit evidence that earth-bound animals will exist after physical death. But it does provide the foundation for a compelling

theological case that God has more in mind for animals than their short sojourn here on Earth.

There are many other evidences I'll add to support this. The most compelling is the biblical and scientific evidence that animals possess souls. If they do, and if God gives their souls immortality, there is no legitimate biblical reason to deny them a future abode in Heaven.

Understanding this watershed issue is so important that it will be the subject of the next three chapters. We'll begin by examining the *scientific* evidence that animals, like humans, have immaterial minds *distinct* from their physical brains—the fundamental qualification for possessing a soul. Following this we'll examine specific biblical evidence for animal souls.

Part One

Scientific and Biblical Evidence for Animal Immortality

CHAPTER 2

What Do Recent Studies in Animal Behavior Reveal? More Than You Might Imagine!

Because animals don't speak a language we can understand, we have assumed they don't feel grief or longing. We've assumed they have little or no memory, can't conceive of the future, or possess self-awareness. There are some people who still think animals don't feel pain! I intend to prove there's not such a great gulf between us.[1]

NOVELIST ANGELA HUNT

Prior to the 19th century, animals were generally regarded as little more than biological machines. Rene Descartes and other 17th century philosophers and scientists even believed animals do not feel pain, which, as novelist Angela Hunt suggests in the above epigraph, some apparently still do. Among other things, this resulted in the cruel practice of vivisection, where experiments and surgery were performed on live animals without anesthesia. Descartes may have justified this practice because he believed animals "have no thought. . . . If they thought as we do, they would have an immortal soul like us."[2] Ironically—and unwittingly—Descartes stated an actual fact. We'll see in later chapters that sentient animals

(animals able to consciously perceive and feel things) *do* have thoughts and *do* possess souls!

Today, it's hard to imagine anyone ever believing that animals have no thoughts, let alone not feel pain. During the last century, an enormous amount of data has been accumulated on animal behavior through the new science of ethology (a branch of biology that studies animal behavior). It's widely recognized today that animals not only feel pain and retain memories of it, but they also engage in thought-driven behaviors and experience real emotions. Senior writer for *Time Magazine*, Jeffrey Kluger, comments on this in his survey of *The Animal Mind*:

> The more deeply scientists look into the animal mind, the more they're discovering it to be a place of richness, joy, thought and even nuance. . . .
>
> Animals, the research is proving, are creatures capable of reflection, bliss, worry and more. Not all of them in the same ways or to the same degrees, surely, but all of them in far deeper measures than we've ever believed. The animal mind is nothing like the wasteland it's been made out to be.[3]

Professor Marc Bekoff, one of the world's leading authorities on animal emotions and cognitive behavior, agrees:

> New studies are producing information that shows just how fascinating and complex animal behavior can be. Animals who seem incapable of much thought have been shown to have remarkable cognitive skills. . . . Many individual . . . animals show distinct personalities and idiosyncratic quirks, just as humans do. There are extroverts, introverts, agreeable individuals, and neurotic animals. . . . There is now mounting evidence that joy, love, grief, jealousy, and

embarrassment, for example, are all experienced by individuals of many species.[4]

Along this same line, ecologist Carl Safina, who has done extensive research into animal behavior, writes about the presence of "personalities" among a wide spectrum of animal species—including not only many mammals and birds, but other animals most of us would never imagine having a personality, such as mice and rats, fish and crabs, and even some varieties of insects and spiders.[5]

So it turns out that what many pet owners intuitively knew all along is true—animals can have *real* emotions, and their behaviors are often deliberate, flexible, and *not* motivated by instinct. "A variety of studies," Bekoff writes, "show that even regular folks (as opposed to trained scientists) can do a consistently accurate job of identifying animal emotions. . . . Whether people are observing wolves, dogs, or cats, they discern emotions nearly as well as trained researchers."[6]

We'll look at specific examples of animal emotions and cognitive abilities in the following chapter. But first, in this chapter, we need to understand what is *not the source* of these mental activities.

Anthropomorphism

When people say their pets are "embarrassed," "feel guilty," or "act sympathetic," critics are quick to call foul and accuse them of being *anthropomorphic*—projecting human emotions, feelings, and thoughts onto animals. It is true that most pet owners probably engage in some level of anthropomorphism—and there is nothing wrong with it. People are comforted and encouraged when they believe their pets are showing affection, sympathy, and genuine concern. Similarly, infirmed and elderly patients are delighted and cheered when "therapy" dogs and cats visit nursing homes and hospitals.

On the other hand, scientists who study animal behavior (ethologists) must constantly be alert to the danger of projecting human characteristics—or their own thoughts and feelings—onto the animals they study. This is crucial in order to avoid misinterpreting animal behavior. Thus, ethologists strive to be completely objective in their field observations and laboratory studies.

Be this as it may, even if pet owners, zookeepers, or professional ethologists do sometimes engage in misdirected anthropomorphism, it does not negate the fact that animals possess genuine emotions and thought processes analogous to humans. The emotions and behaviors observed in many animal species cannot be attributed solely to the observers' anthropomorphic assumptions. To claim otherwise is not only unwarranted reductionism, but it flies in the face of modern studies in animal behavior. As a matter of fact, according Professor Bekoff, the best way for researchers to accurately describe and explain animal thoughts, feelings, and behaviors is through anthropomorphic language:

> Many researchers have ignored what is so very obvious—we are humans and we have, by necessity, a human view of the world. The way we describe and explain the behavior of other animals is limited by the language we use to talk about things in general. By engaging in anthropomorphism, we make other animals' worlds accessible to ourselves and to other human beings. . . .
>
> Being anthropomorphic is unavoidable because we have to use human languages and experiences to meaningfully describe and explain animal behavior and animal feelings. . . . [I]t allows other animals' behavior and emotions to be accessible to us. . . . Anthropomorphism can help make accessible to us the behavior and thoughts and feelings of animals with whom we are sharing a particular experience.[7]

In other words, anthropomorphism is an important tool for understanding and describing these mental states. Commenting on Bekoff's study, theologian and scholar Richard Bauckham adds this:

> Renouncing anthropomorphism altogether is bound to be reductionist, explaining animal behaviour in wholly mechanistic terms. To use anthropomorphic language need not imply that we recognize no difference between our own feelings and those of animals; only that we postulate something similar on the basis of the behaviour we observe. . . . Bekoff argues for the scientific use of anthropomorphism provided it is used carefully and "biocentrically," meaning that we make every attempt to understand who animals are in their own world.[8]

Perhaps a fair analogy can be made with how God communicates with humans. Just as ethologists use anthropomorphic language to understand and describe animal thoughts and emotions, God uses human language to communicate His holiness and divine messages in a way that humans can understand. Theologian J. I. Packer explains:

> Biblical statements about God's jealousy are *anthropomorphism*— that is, descriptions of God in language drawn from the life of man. The Bible is full of anthropomorphisms—God's arm, hand, and finger, His hearing, seeing, and smelling, His tenderness, anger, repentance, laughter, joy, and so forth. The reason why God uses these terms to speak to us about Himself is that language drawn from our own personal life is the most accurate medium for communicating thoughts about Him that we have.[9]

Passages such as Genesis 6:6, "The Lord was sorry that He had made man on the earth," and Exodus 32:14, "the Lord changed His mind" (NASB), are obviously intended to communicate God's grief and response to human failures in a way that people could identify with and understand. But from the divine perspective, God didn't literally change His mind or was "sorry" in the human understandings of the words. That would be impossible for a sovereign, omniscient God. Similarly, in Genesis 3:8-11, when Adam and Eve hid in the Garden and God called out to them "Where are you?" He knew exactly where they were and why they were hiding. It was a way for the infinite, sovereign God to play out the scenario in human terms. In like manner, in order for us to fully understand and explain how many animals think, feel, and emote, we are forced to engage in a measure of careful anthropomorphism and use anthropomorphic language.

Personally, I don't believe it takes a professional ethologist to recognize genuine animal emotions. It is not being anthropomorphic to look into the doleful eyes of a chained dog and determine it's feeling sad. Nor is it anthropomorphic to watch a caged zoo animal pace restlessly back and forth and recognize it's frustrated and bored. Still, we must balance these legitimate conclusions against the pitfall of wrongly projecting human feelings, emotions, and reasoning abilities on pets and other animals that go beyond their inherent capabilities. As I see it, there are three ways to avoid this.

First, we must recognize that human-like traits observable in animals are far less developed and manifested than they are in people. But this does not mean they *don't* exist. Animal mental states do not perfectly reflect humans', and for a very good reason. Only humans are created in the divine image (Gen. 1:27), and only people have an exalted position in creation (see Ps. 8:4–6). God did not create animals for the same purposes as He did humans, nor did He endow them with the same lofty degree of self-awareness and free will. So when pets and wild animals experience grief or joy, or some other human-like emotion, it will never be identical to the same experiences in humans. We should not read more into the behavior of pets and wild animals than they are capable of experiencing.

Second, we must recognize that human-like traits found in animals must be *innate* to the animals themselves—regardless of whether or not *Homo sapiens* possess similar traits. It may come as a surprise, but qualities such as memory, reasoning, empathy, anticipation, frustration, boredom, sadness, grief, joy, and other mental activities are innate characteristics of many animal species (as we'll see in the following chapter).

Instinct

The third thing to keep in mind, in order to avoid projecting human thoughts and feelings on animals, is not to confuse *instinctive* behavior with self-directed mental activities. Instinct causes an animal to involuntarily and automatically respond in a particular way to outside (or internal) influences or stimuli, as opposed to responding freely and with a measure of flexibility. To put this scientifically, God placed within the gene pool of all animal species certain innate traits that ensure their survival and success in propagating the species. Instinctive behavior is usually centered on fight/flight reactions, reproductive behaviors, and migratory patterns. It is less pronounced in so-called "higher" animals (i.e. mammals and birds)—where learned behavior can sometimes trump instinct.

Animals do not have the brain capacity to reason and think anywhere near the level of humans, and therefore no animal species could survive without the safety net of instinct. In terms of anthropomorphism, we must be careful not to confuse instinctive behavior with more self-directed activities. When a tomcat is howling outside a bedroom window in the middle of the night, or fighting another male in the backyard, it is not a romantic serenade or a desire to bully a weaker tomcat. It's merely the instinct to mate and chase off competitors.

Collecting the Evidence

Field studies of wild animals are essential in order to collect data that can't be gathered in laboratories or zoos, and most of what follows in the next chapter depends largely on such research. As the late Nobel Prize winning naturalist Konrad Lorenz wrote, "It is only by living with animals that one can attain a real understanding of their ways"[10]

An enormous amount of insight into animal thoughts and emotions has also been accumulated through behavioral studies of our canine companions. According to the American Veterinary Medical Association, over forty-three million American households have at least one dog. This translates into nearly seventy million canine pets.[11] As professor Bekoff further observed, "To live with a dog is to know firsthand that animals have feelings. It's a no-brainer. . . . I know no practicing researcher who doesn't attribute emotions to their companion animals."[12] In the following chapter, I'll also refer to behavioral studies of dogs.

There is another avenue of animal observations that has gained credible scientific approval in recent years: wildlife rescue centers and other private animal sanctuaries, where injured, orphaned, and abandoned wild and domesticated animals are sheltered and cared for—sometimes for many years. Animal caretakers in these facilities provide tremendous data from long-term observations of the animals under their care. This has prompted many ethologists to increasingly consider animal shelters as valuable resources for animal behavior studies.

A *Nature* documentary aired on public television in December, 2012, "Animal Odd Couples" (which included an interview with Marc Bekoff), emphasized the value of animal care facilities as a source of reliable "field studies." Although the animals are not living in their native habitats, these facilities still provide important information on animal behavior. As the documentary pointed out, when a hundred observations of a particular behavior is repeated over and over, it's extremely likely it reflects an animal's normal behavior in the wilds.

Mind Verses Brain

If animal thoughts and emotions cannot be fully accounted for through instinct or fanciful anthropomorphisms, where do they originate? I believe the evidence shows that animal emotions and other mental activities originate the same way they do in humans— in their *minds*.

I explore this in detail in appendix one because it's significant and compelling evidence for life after death for both animals *and* humans. However, this takes us into the fascinating realm of brain science, and I don't want to get sidetracked from the issue at hand. I'll continue the mind verses brain discussion in the appendix and only touch on what is relevant for now.

The watershed issue of whether or not humans and animals will live on in Heaven is whether or not they have souls. And the fundamental feature of a soul is an immaterial (non-physical) mind that exists *distinct* from a physical brain. In humans, our mind is the seat of our intellect, emotions, and will. It is that faculty of our being that survives physical death and lives on in our soul, once it departs our body at death. Therefore, it's reasonable to assume that animals with minds, that is, animals with emotions and cognitive abilities similar to humans, must also possess souls that can survive physical death. (In chapter four, I'll demonstrate that the Bible unequivocally teaches that animals *do* have souls.)

The primary evidence that many animals have minds—and thus potentially *immortal* souls—is that they possess mental capabilities that in humans can *only* be attributed to non-physical (immaterial) minds. As pointed out, current research in animal behavior reveals that many characteristics once thought to distinguish *Homo sapiens* from animals have clear parallels in nonhuman life. Numerous animals have emotions, feelings, and even thought-driven behaviors similar to soul-bearing humans—although, understandably, much less developed than in humans. This provides compelling evidence that *at least* sentient animals (animals that can consciously perceive and feel things) have minds. Since in humans, our mind is a property of our soul and survives physical death, we have every reason to believe that animals with minds also have souls that will survive physical death. (At this point I'm not concerned about whether or not animal souls will be reunited with resurrected bodies. That will be the topic of part three.)

In the following chapter, we'll look at some of the most obvious and well-attested emotions and thought-driven (cognitive) behaviors observed in many species of animals, which correspond to similar thoughts and emotions in humans. We'll focus on two kinds of data. We'll examine studies of wild animals in their native habitats and current research on domestic dogs. Together they will demonstrate beyond doubt that animals *do* possess mental abilities characteristic of soul-bearing humans.

CHAPTER 3

What Do Animals Think, Feel, and Experience?

John Steinbeck wrote a delightful book about traveling around America with his dog, Charley. In the book (appropriately titled *Travels with Charley*), Steinbeck described a bizarre incident where his otherwise docile and cowardly poodle encountered a bear. Unexpectedly, Charley made a sudden, frightening transition from an "old, calm friend" into a raving, ranting, ferocious "maniac." After marveling at Charley's seemingly inexplicable behavior, Steinbeck wrote, "I wonder why we think the thoughts and emotions of animals are simple."[1]

Steinbeck was right to ponder the wonder of animal thoughts and emotions because they truly are remarkable—and far more complex than most people realize. The fact is many animals have emotions, feelings, and the capacity to think and understand in ways that closely parallel similar characteristic in humans.

In the following pages, we'll examine some of the most amazing and insightful examples of animal emotions and cognition.[2] As pointed out in the previous chapter, this is powerful and compelling evidence that sentient animals, like humans, have immaterial minds and thus potentially *immortal* souls.

Emotions and Feelings

Novelist Dean Koontz, who is a Christian, is not a professional ethologist. But he makes an insightful observation, which many pet owners will agree, in his delightful book, *A Big Little Life* (which all dog lovers should read). After nearly a decade of friendship with a remarkable Golden Retriever named Trixie, Koontz observed: "As anyone who has ever opened his heart and mind to a dog knows, these creatures have emotions very like our own."[3]

Professional ethologists agree with Koontz. Marc Bekoff writes: "There is every reason to believe that many animals [including dogs] feel just as many emotions as humans do." Moreover, he adds, it's not difficult to recognize basic emotions in animals. "All we have to do is look, listen, and smell. Their faces, their eyes, and the ways in which they carry themselves can be used to make strong inference about what they are feeling."[4]

What kinds of human-like emotions do animals experience? Here are some examples.

Altruism, Devotion, Loyalty, Friendship

Ethologists who study wild animals in their native habitats often observe members of a pack or herd forging strong bonds with one another that go well beyond survival instinct. Many acts of altruism, devotion, loyalty, and even lasting friendships have been observed among various animal species.

A fascinating article in the London *Telegraph* described mounting evidence that wolves, coyotes, elephants, bats, whales, and other animals "appear to have an innate sense of fairness, display empathy and help other animals that are in distress." For example, "elephants are intensely sociable and emotional animals. . . . In one case, a Matriarch known as Eleanor fell ill and a female in the herd gently tried to help Eleanor back to her feet, staying with her before she died." Similarly, the article continues, "experiments with domestic dogs, where one animal was given a treat and another denied, have shown that they possess a sense of fairness as they shared their treats." Even rodents have displayed altruistic behaviors. "Experiments with rats have shown that they will not take food if they know their actions will cause pain to another rat." Although not as pleasant to visualize, the *Telegraph* article also reports that vampire bats "who are successful in foraging for blood will share their meal with bats who are not successful."[5]

Strong and lasting friendships are common among many other animal species, including chimps, baboons, horses, hyenas, and dolphins. What's less well-known is that devotion and friendships can also be *interspecies*. Numerous instances of one species of animal forming a close relationship with an entirely *different* species of animal have been observed, sometimes even between predator and prey![6] In her book *Unlikely Friendships*, senior writer for *National Geographic*, Jennifer Holland, described nearly fifty examples of "unlikely" interspecies "friendships," including an African lioness and baby oryx, an elephant and stray dog, and a leopard and cow.[7]

The *Telegraph* article mentioned above provides several examples of interspecies acts of altruism and loyalty. One of my favorites is the account of a herd of eleven elephants in South Africa that rescued antelopes being held inside an enclosure. A particularly touching story was reported in a San Diego newspaper. It described a Doberman Pinscher in Florida that had been missing for fifteen hours. It had either jumped or fallen over a seawall and became stranded on a sandbar, with the tide rising. A group of dolphins, which had apparently been watching over the dog, alerted passing vacationers by splashing water to create a "big commotion." Because of their efforts, the dog was rescued and reunited with its owners.[8] Just as amazing are the countless stories of dolphins rescuing *people* at sea. "From antiquity to recent times," writes researcher Carl Safina, "stories of dolphins pushing distressed swimmers to the surface are too numerous to track."[9] Dolphin rescue stories include pods of dolphins protecting swimmers from attack by great white sharks![10]

Even more remarkable are encounters between humans and potentially dangerous animals. "Three lions in Ethiopia," relates Bekoff, "rescued a twelve-year-old girl from a gang who had kidnapped her. Said Sergeant Wondimu Wedajo: 'They stood guard until we found her and then they just left her like a gift and went back into the forest.'"[11] Orcas (aka, killer whales) are thought to be one of the most dangerous animals to hunt the seas (although there has never been a case of a killer whale attacking a human in the ocean). "The fact is" writes Safina, "killer whales seem capable of random acts of kindness." In his book *Beyond Words,* he recounts several stories of killer whales retrieving lost dogs and rescuing people lost at sea.[12]

When it comes to acts of devotion and loyalty, few accounts surpass human/dog relationships. One of the most incredible is the story of a dog named *Hachi,* narrated in the movie of the same name. (The movie took place in America, but it's based on a true story that occurred in Japan.) As the movie unfolds, a distinguished scholar named Parker Wilson (played by Richard Gere) befriends a lost Akita puppy, which becomes his friend and companion. As an adult dog, Hachi developed the habit of waiting at the train station every day for Wilson to return home. Sadly, the college professor suddenly died of a heart attack. For many years thereafter, until his own death, Hachi returned every day to the train station to await the professor's return home. (A monument in Japan at the site of Hachi's vigilance testifies to his devotion to his friend.) Could Hachi's behavior be attributed to instinct? Not likely. It was his loyalty and devotion to his human companion that drew Hachi to the train station every day for years after Parker Wilson's death.

Nowhere are accounts of animal devotion and loyalty to humans more moving and poignant than stories about service dogs. Sometimes their selfless acts go far beyond what one would expect under the circumstance. Pastor Mike Macintosh wrote a book about his experiences as a chaplain at Ground Zero, after the tragic collapse of the Twin Towers. One chapter describes three dog stories that epitomize the selfless devotion of these remarkable animals. In one amazing case, a Golden Labrador guide dog, named Rosella, led her master to safety through the horrifying carnage of the burning Towers. Macintosh recounts: "I couldn't help but focus on this dog and wonder what had been at work inside her that day that allowed her to bring her master down more than seventy stories in a burning building? How did she ignore all the distractions, all the noise and frantic people hurtling past her? She definitely had discipline for her job and *devotion for her master* (emphasis added).[13]

Grief, Loneliness, Sadness, and Mourning
Animal emotions are also displayed in feelings of grief, loneliness, sadness, and mourning. During the past few decades, a considerable amount of research has accumulated from field studies, zoos, wildlife sanctuaries, and pet owners that demonstrate this. Cognitive ethologist Bekoff describes animal grief as remarkably similar to humans:

> Grieving animals may withdraw from their group and seek seclusion, resistant to all attempts by others to draw them out. They may sit in one place, motionless, staring vacantly into space. They stop eating and lose interest in sex. Sometimes they become obsessed with the dead individual. They may try to revive him or her, and failing that, remain with the carcass for days on end.[14]

Hachi's years of unwearied devotion was likely prompted by grief and loneliness after Parker Wilson died. My wife's dog Bear visibly displayed his loneliness when my family was on vacation. In two separate instances, his caretakers later told us, he pulled the bedspread off our bed, dragged it into the living room, and spent most of his day lying on top of it. Apparently, our lingering scent brought him a degree of comfort in our absence.

Perhaps the most striking and best attested examples of animal grief and sadness are observed among elephants. It is well documented that elephants are highly sensitive to the suffering of other elephants, and even death.[15] It's not unusual for a family of elephants to return to the body of a deceased member for many days.

Bekoff relates the story of an elephant named Sissy, who lived in the Elephant Sanctuary in Tennessee. Sissy had a favorite tire she carried around as a "security blanket." After her friend Tina (another elephant) died, Sissy left her tire at the gravesite and stood vigilant for two days.[16] Another researcher, who has worked a half century raising orphaned elephants, concluded that elephants can even *die* of grief.[17]

Besides elephants, a variety of other animals clearly display the emotions of grief and mourning. Researcher Jeffrey Kluger gives examples of dogs, cats, horses, rabbits, gorillas, chimps, bonobos, and baboons (the latter four have been observed carrying around their dead babies, even to the start of decomposition). Perhaps his most striking and unusual example of animals showing signs of mourning are from a species most of us would never expect to display such an emotion: crows.

> An animal that inflicts death so readily seems deeply moved when one if its own kind dies. A dead crow lying in the open will quickly attract two or three other crows. They dive and swoop and scold, emitting a very particular call

that summons up to a hundred other members of the flock. [Crows possess over 200 distinct calls with different meanings.] With near ceremonial coordination, they land and surround the body, often in complete silence. Some may bring sticks or bits of grass and lay them next to—or even on top of—the remains. Then, tribute paid, they turn and fly off.[18]

That many varieties of animals experience grief and mourning at the death of a friend, mate, or baby further illustrates the striking emotional similarities between humans and numerous sentient animals.

Compassion and Empathy

Two other emotions that sentient animals share with humans are compassion and empathy. As with the previous examples of human-like emotions, illustrations of animals displaying these two emotions are near endless. Professor Bekoff relates a touching account of compassion while observing a group of wild elephants in the Samburu Reserve, Northern Kenya. One of the elephants was crippled and could not keep up with the rest of the herd. The other elephants, however, would not let her get behind. They would stop, look around to see where she was, and often wait for her to catch up. This went on for years![19]

Jeffrey Kluger reports on a study done at the Yerkes National Primate Research Center in Atlanta that also illustrates animal compassion. It "showed that when capuchin monkeys were offered a choice between two tokens—one that would buy two slices of apple and one that would buy one slice each for them and a partner monkey—they chose the generous option, provided the partner was a relative or at least familiar to them."[20]

Naturalist and pioneer animal behaviorist in the mid-twentieth century, the late Konrad Lorenz, gives a humorous illustration of animal empathy in his classic book *King Solomon's Ring*, which explores "the human side of birds and animals." He wrote that his dog knew "exactly which people got on my nerves, and when. Nothing could prevent her from biting, gently but surely, all such people on their posteriors."[21] Was this instinct or empathy? I have no doubt it was the dog's ability to understand and share Lorenz's feelings—a fine example of animal empathy played out within the limits of a dog's ability to express it.

Compassionate and empathetic behavior is not particularly rare in the animal kingdom. It has been observed not only among acknowledged intelligent animals, such as elephants, monkeys, dolphins, and dogs, but also among presumably less intelligent animals. The journal *Science* reported a series of experiments by neuroscientists that "demonstrated that mice suffer significantly more distress when they saw a familiar mouse suffering than when they saw the same kind of pain in a stranger. . . . 'This is a highly significant finding and should open the eyes of people who think empathy is limited to our species.'"[22]

My wife and I recently witnessed a sweet example of empathy in our newest canine companion, Maggie—a gentle and affectionate lab/shepherd mix we adopted from a rescue center when she was ten months old. Maggie loves to watch television documentaries about dogs and wildlife. (She rarely shows any interest in human-focused programs, dozing through the most exciting scenes.) I recently timed her watching a show on Yellowstone wolves. She unerringly watched the program for forty minutes, seldom glancing away from the screen. This was amazing enough, but in a scene where some wolf pups were frightened and crying, Maggie became restless and began to whine with them. This wasn't the first time she exhibited emphatic behavior. A few weeks previously she and my wife were watching a television program where a veterinarian was attempting to save several dying puppies. When the pups began to cry, Maggie immediately became agitated. She stood up, paced back and forth, and cried out in distress and sympathy for the puppies.

Do dogs have emotions and feelings similar to humans? Maggie poignantly demonstrated feelings of compassion, empathy, and sadness, defining characteristics of humans—and many sentient animals.

Do These Traits Suggest a Moral Conscience in Animals?

I need to add something here before continuing. When we talk about animals demonstrating compassion, empathy, loyalty, altruism, and other characteristics that seem to imply a sense of moral consciousness, we shouldn't think of it entirely in human terms. Humans are unique in the sense that we alone are created in God's image and as such are moral beings with a God-given moral conscience (Rom. 2:14-15). Animals do not possess a clear moral awareness of what ought to be as distinct from what ought not to be—in a human understanding of what constitutes acceptable moral behavior. A dominant bull elk or stallion will seek to mate with as many females in their respective harems as possible; resisting promiscuity is not a moral obligation in animals (although some varieties of animals do faithfully mate for life). Similarly, birds drawn to the feeders in our yard are often unwilling to share the bounty, and instead bicker and chase each other away from the food. The point is, what humans think of as moral behavior will not be found among animals where instinct dominates certain activities. Nevertheless, characteristics of compassion, empathy, loyalty, altruism, and so on are all observable among many sentient animals.

These behaviors seem to be motivated in ways that violate evolutionary expectations, which suggests that animal behavior would never include activities that threatens an individual's or a group's welfare or survival. But as I've shown, animal behavior often trumps instinct and is expressed in ways that are clearly beyond self-interest and survival of the fittest. Many sentient animals display unique behaviors that appear to exhibit a degree of moral-like integrity—even if they are not on the level of human moral consciousness.

With this said, let's continue looking at examples of animals emotions and feelings.

Joy and Pleasure

On the brighter side of animal emotions are displays of joy and pleasure. Just as with humans, these emotions are most clearly expressed in play, which is a characteristic in almost all species of mammals and many varieties of birds.[23] Anyone who has watched wildlife footage on television documentaries (or raised a dog or cat) is familiar with the fun-filled antics of numerous animal species. Scenes of adults (not just adolescents) romping in the snow, sliding on ice, tumbling down grassy hillsides, playing "tag," and wrestling with each other for the sheer joy of it are clear indications that such behaviors are motivated by more than instinct—such activities are just plain fun!

The same can be said about animal joy. As Jeffrey Kluger observed in his book *The Animal Mind,* "There is no reason to believe that a dog assuming a play pose or a herd of elephants trumpeting at a reunion do not experience much of the same joy we do when we behave in similar ways. As with us, too, the very act of expressing that Joy—through our cheers, hugs, whoops and words—make the feelings more powerful still."[24]

Play is not the only way animals exhibit joy and pleasure, as most pet owners readily acknowledged. When taken for a walk, especially when released from a leash, dogs make an immediate transition from backyard boredom to tireless fun-filled explorers. I described above how Maggie loves to watch television shows about animals. Her willingness to focus for so long on a television documentary about wolves can only be attributed to the fact that it was pleasurable (other than when the wolf pups were crying). Why else would she concentrate so intensely for forty uninterrupted minutes on something that provided no scent, offered no physical contact, and with no body language or other communication directed toward her? Maggie simply *enjoyed* watching the show!

Affection and Love

Many sentient animals are social creatures and need affection and companionship the same as humans. Animal "love," writes Professor Bekoff, can be identified as "preferring the close company of another individual, seeking them out, and if necessary protecting and caring for them. It means forming and maintaining strong and close reciprocal social bonds and communicating feelings between loved ones." Drawing from this definition, Bekoff asserts, "There's considerable evidence that many animals are capable of feelings that run the gamut of the varieties of love, and the latest science argues for the existence of love in many different species."[25]

Author Ted Kerasote wrote a beautiful and sensitive book on the world of dogs, which he developed around the life of his canine friend, Merle. The book also includes insightful research on other members of the canine family. Among other things, Kerasote's research showed that "dogs who were hand fed by attendants immediately lost interest in their keepers if they were shown no affection. On the other hand, dogs became attached to people who lavished affection upon them even when these people did not feed them." Moreover, he continues, "Innumerable case studies have shown that the large increase in dysfunctional canine behavior, especially aggression, is a direct result of more and more dogs living solitary lives."[26]

My wife and I experienced firsthand the power of love in overcoming a serious dysfunction with our rescued dog, Maggie. Although we know little about her first ten months of life, she was clearly abused. When she came to live with us, she had been so traumatized and mistreated that she didn't even know how to play. In particular, she avoided any contact with men—including me for the first few weeks (leading us to believe it was a man who abused her). But after several months of constant love and affection she began to change. Today, more than a year later, she has become one of the most lovable and playful dogs we know—including with men.

It's a rare pet owner who doesn't believe his or her furry companion is capable of affection and love. But is this anthropomorphic sentimentality on our part—or is it genuine feelings of love for their human companions? Responding to the question, "Does my dog love me, or does he just want a treat," researcher Carl Safina answers the question with an emphatic, *yes*:

> Short answer: your dog really does love you. Part of the reason is: because you are kind. If you were abusive, your dog would fear you. And they might *still* love you, out of duty or need—not so different from many people trapped in abusive relationships. But to answer the question directly: what we know about dogs' brain . . . tells us that yes, your dog loves you. . . . No matter how [dogs' love] originated, their feelings are real to them. Your dog genuinely loves you, as you . . . love your dog.[27]

Now, when it comes to fully understanding what love and affection mean to animals, we must be careful not to humanize the concept. Love and affection (and the other emotions we examined) can't be thought of as being directly equivalent to similar human emotions. If a dog or elephant expresses love or joy, it will be dog-love and dog-joy and elephant-love and elephant-joy, not human love and joy. Animal emotions can only be expressed within the mental capabilities and physical makeup of the animal. But that they are not human-like in intensity or complexity does not mean they do not exist. The same is also true in terms of animal cognition, which we turn to next.

Animal Cognition and Thought-Driven Behavior

Cognition is the mental ability to acquire and understand knowledge through thought, experience, and the senses. In the animal world, just as with humans, this entails the ability to learn, to remember what has been learned, to communicate it to others, and, for some animals, to have a degree of self-awareness.

Learning

It was long assumed that animals were incapable of much thought and functioned mostly on instinct. It's now widely known that many species have astonishing cognitive skills. Mammals and birds in particular are capable of gaining knowledge and understanding, can learn to respond with flexibility to environmental and other challenges, and can retain memories that guide their future behavior. A sad but good example of this is reported by awarding-winning wildlife conservation journalist, Glen Martin:

> [A] herd of elephants . . . had been terrorizing a farming hamlet, intimidating the residents, and laying waste to their pumpkin patches. After unsuccessfully trying to rout the animals with nonlethal means . . . [it was] determined that

shooting one of the dominant adults was the best way to drive the group off. . . .

"[T]he plan worked—the herd completely left the area. They understand what it means when one of them is shot."[28]

It was also long assumed that one of the criteria that distinguished humans from animals was the ability to use tools. Jane Goodall's work with Chimpanzees proved otherwise. Today, it is well known that chimps and other primates fashion and use tools, and most people are familiar with sea otters smashing clams with rocks. What isn't well-known is that many other animals also use tools. Elephants, dolphins, birds, octopuses, and even wasps, ants and some other insects use tools. Satin Bowerbirds have been observed using fibrous pieces of bark, which they soak with berry juice, to paint the inside of their bowers.[29] Crows and ravens are two of the most intelligent, adaptive, and innovative members of the avian clan.[30] (Relative to body weight, ravens have the same size brain as chimpanzee's.) They can identify and remember individual *human* faces and are capable of manufacturing tools. For example, crows have been observed constructing and manipulating tools out of "sticks, leaves, wires, strings and any other natural or artificial object. . . . They find just the right twigs, crack them free of the branch, and then twist the twig ends into needle-sharp hooks. . . . With these hooks and their spears they extract slugs, insects and other invertebrates from deep crevices in the ground or in trees."[31]

Here are a few other examples of animals using tools. Recently a young brown bear in Alaska's Glacier Bay National Park became the first of its kind ever observed using a tool. A researcher reported in the journal *Animal Cognition* that the animal was observed "repeatedly picking up barnacle-encrusted rocks in shallow water, manipulated and reoriented them in its forepaws, and used them to rub its neck and muzzle."[32] African elephants have been observed dropping large branches, and sometimes entire trees, on electrically charged fences, which are designed to keep them out of agricultural areas. Somehow, they learned that this will short out the fences and allow them to pass through without being shocked. Egyptian Vultures provide yet another remarkable example of tool use. They are known to drop stones to crack open the tough shells of ostrich eggs, which are thick enough to support their 300 pound parents.

Although relatively few species of animals are known to use tools, many exhibit an amazing capacity to learn, sometimes simply by *observing* other animals struggling to solve problems in a trial-and-error fashion. Researcher Ted Kerasote commented on this: "Animals can learn by observing other animals and then apply what they've seen to themselves without any direct positive or negative reinforcement. In other words, the training is in the watching, not in the doing."[33]

Our dog friends exhibit this trait daily. They are keenly aware of our body language, and, unlike wolves, will look directly into our eyes in order to identify our intentions or possible reactions. They easily discern what we're focused on and even understand when we wordlessly point toward an object—something chimpanzees are unable to comprehend, unless trained.

The ability to learn and pass on knowledge to their offspring is crucial for the survival of many animals. Instinct often plays no role. Elephants must learn practically everything it takes to be an elephant from other elephants during the early years of their lives. Remarkably, this includes being taught to fear lions![34] Similarly, virtually everything young otters learn, including what kinds of food to eat and grooming practices, must be taught by their parents. Newborn otters can do little more than eat, poop, and float.

Konrad Lorenze studied the highly developed social and family life of Jackdaws (a type of small crow) for many years. He reported that communicating how to recognize a potential enemy to young and inexperienced birds "is a real acquired knowledge, not mere innate, instinctive reaction." Referring to animals in general, he adds, "an animal which does not know its enemy by innate instinct, is informed by older and more experienced fellow-members of its species who or what is to be feared as hostile. This is true tradition, the handing-down of personally acquired knowledge from one generation to another."[35]

Along the same line, Lorenz writes about the ability of dogs to learn and communicate their wishes to humans. When a "dog wants to make you open the door or turn on the tap . . . what he does has the specific and purposeful motive of influencing you in a certain direction. . . . The intelligent actions of [dogs] . . . are not innate but are individually learned and governed by true insights."[36]

I had a humorous experience with my wife's dog, Bear, which illustrates a dog's capacity to influence and manipulate their human companions. Bear had injured his dew-claw (the elevated claw at the rear of a dog's foot). Lisa took him to the vet, and upon returning home he acted fine the rest of the day—until I came home. As soon as I walked in the door and expressed my sympathy, Bear immediately leaned against the wall and then slowly limped toward me. He got what he wanted, more sympathy and vigorous petting. Did Bear anticipate my response if he faked an injury?— you bet he did.

Memory

Learning would be of little value unless an animal could apply it by remembering the past and planning for future activities. Bekoff writes, "There are literally volumes of data showing that individuals of many species do think about the future." He illustrates this with examples of several varieties of birds and mammals hiding food for later retrieval, and of subordinate chimpanzees and wolves pretending they don't see a food item if a dominate animal is around—but returning later to eat it.[37] A similar phenomenon has been observed among jays, ravens, and crows. They "appear to intuit what's going on in the minds of other birds, hiding food in one spot when they know they're being observed . . . and then re-hiding it as soon as they're alone."[38] The ability to understand when they are being watched by dominant members—and pretending they don't know it—gives remarkable insight into the intelligence of sentient animals.

Actually, it doesn't take a trained ethologist to know that animals have remarkable memories. Most dog and cat owners are well aware of the abilities of their animal companions to remember past errors that resulted in punishment, as well as behaviors that elicit rewards. Speaking about dogs, cognitive psychologist and animal behaviorist Alexandra Horowitz writes,

> Dogs certainly remember a large amount: they remember their owners, their homes, the place they walk. They remember innumerable other dogs, they know about rain and snow after experiencing them once; they remember where to find a good smell and where to find a good stick. They know when we can't see what they are doing; they remember what made us mad last time they chewed it up; they know when they are allowed on the bed and when they are forbidden from it. They only know these things because they have learned them—and learning is just memory of associations or events over time. . . . They sometimes act as though they are thinking about their own future. . . .
>
> And dogs certainly anticipate what is in their near future.[39]

Dogs also have an incredible ability to learn and remember human words. Many dogs can respond to more than a hundred commands, and in one amazing case a dog named Rico developed a vocabulary of around *two hundred* words![40]

Communication

"For centuries," writes researcher Carl Safina, "the fact that other animals don't converse the way humans do has been interpreted as evidence of empty minds."[41] Scientists now know differently—and it makes perfect sense that God would enable wild creatures to communicate with each other.

If animals can learn and remember, it follows they should be able to communicate this knowledge to other animals. They can. We may not understand them, but many animals speak a "language" using various audible sounds that communicate specific information. Dolphins, whales, elephants, canines, crows, ravens, parrots, apes, and numerous other animals have complex vocabularies and communicate verbally. Other animals "speak" to one another through body language. Specific postures and the position of ears, eyes, tails, and facial expressions are all ways in which animals communicate their emotions and feelings to each other.

Science and nature journalist Jennifer Holland relates a fascinating account of animal communication. Referring to what she describes as "the most famous example of interspecies friendship ever told," she recounts the unlikely relationship between a tortoise and hippo that includes an amazing example of *interspecies* communication:

> Scientists have been most fascinated with how [these] two animals developed their own physical and verbal language. With gentle nips and nudges to feet or tails, they told each other when to move and in which direction. They sounded off, back and forth, with deep rumbling sounds not typical of either animals. "What strikes me is how sophisticated

their mutual communication system became," says animal behaviorist Barbara King. "It's a dynamic dance between two species with no present program on how to deal with each other. And it can't just be instinct, because one was shaping its behavior to the other."[42]

Self-Awareness

We now come to the most controversial cognitive ability displayed in some sentient animals: self-awareness—a consciousness of their *own* feelings, motivations, and desires. Many ethologists believe dogs, apes, elephants, and other vertebrates, including some birds, are self-aware—not, of course, in the same way or to the same degree as humans.

We've seen that numerous animal species have emotions, express deep feelings, and engage in thought-driven behaviors. They can learn and pass on important knowledge, make changes if they error, retain memories that determine how they will respond to future events and circumstances, and are able to clearly communicate with one another. All these human-like mental activities seem to imply the likelihood that at least some animals are self-aware, that is, they recognize themselves as distinct from other animals and their surrounding environments.

Writing about animal pain, C. S. Lewis declared his "strong conviction" that "higher animals, and specially in those we tame" possess "a real, though doubtless rudimentary, selfhood."[43] Scientific studies increasingly support Lewis' insight, and ethologists generally agree that many animals have a sense of self. Consider this article in the science section of a large metropolitan newspaper:

Humans have somewhat arrogantly maintained that they are the only creatures to be self-aware. . . . But recent studies have demonstrated that dolphins, some species of primates and elephants can recognize and react to their own reflections. . . . Macaques [a genus of monkeys] . . . placed in front of mirrors soon come to realize they are looking at themselves and not other monkeys. . . . They began performing gymnastic feats to view their reflections and to see otherwise inaccessible parts of their bodies. This behavior stopped when the mirror was covered up.[44]

Studies have shown similar responses to the "mirror test" among dolphins. When encountering mirrors, dolphins will examine their teeth and engage in different motions, such as rolling over and shaking their head back and forth. This is best explained as evidence of self-awareness. Dogs, adds Horowitz, also show "behaviors suggestive of their self-knowledge."[45] Bekoff agrees: "It is obvious to most pet owners that their companion animals are self-cognizant to some degree [certainly self-aware, and perhaps even self-conscious]" (brackets part of quote).[46]

Carl Safina adds an additional insight into the mirror test that's worth noting, making it even more significant as a measurement for self-awareness: "Ironically," he writes, "mirror-test enthusiasts overlook what's perhaps the most interesting thing: understanding reflection means that you understand that the reflection is not *you;* you understand that it *represents* you. Fathoming 'representation' means that the mirror gazer's mind has *symbolic* abilities . . . [which] demonstrates rare abductive reasoning" (making a logical inference).[47] I agree with Safina that this is far more significant, in terms of animal self-awareness and intelligence, than the standard interpretation of the mirror test.

Determining to what degree various animal species possess an actual sense of self may always remain elusive, if not impossible. Nevertheless, within the limitations of their individual mental capabilities, it seems likely that at least some animals are self-aware. Why is this significant? Because, more than any other mental activity, self-awareness cannot be reduced to mere instinct. It requires independent thinking, imagination, and even *abstract* thoughts. Environmental reporter Glen Martin provides a fitting summary on animal self-awareness:

> [T]he concept of "awareness" as a uniquely human quality is a canard [unfounded rumor]. Increasingly, we are learning that animals are capable of both ratiocination [making judgments by a process of logic or reason] and emotional subtlety: that many species think and feel deeply, that they play, that they love. And not just bonbos and chimps. The other great apes, elephants, cetaceans [whales, dolphins, porpoises], wolves, and hyenas, not to mention African gray parrots and other psittacines [birds in the parrot family]— ethologists are finding that all these species express a deep and complicated suite of cognitive and emotional responses.
>
> In other words, they are intelligent and sentient, not in precisely the same way humans are, perhaps, but intelligent and sentient nonetheless. Indeed, recent research indicates some animals share certain emotive processes with human beings.[48]

What does all this cumulative research from decades of field studies by skilled ethologists, animal sanctuary staff, laboratory observations by trained scientists, and the anecdotal observations of pet owners teach us? It reveals that many animals possess emotional and cognitive characteristics that reflect intelligence, feelings, and intentional thought-driven behaviors that are remarkably similar to humans. Thus, modern studies in animal behavior sufficiently demonstrate that at least sentient animals, like humans, *have minds.*

Moreover, as explained in the previous chapter (and developed in appendix one), in humans our mind is the essential property of our soul. Is it legitimate, then, to conclude that animals also possess souls? Logically and scientifically the answer seems to be, yes. But the ultimate answer to this question can only be ascertained by biblical revelation. So, what does God say about this? Do animals have souls? And if so, did God given them *immortal* souls, as He did with humans? This brings us to chapter four.

CHAPTER 4

Animals Have Souls, but Are They Immortal Souls?

The world's most famous veterinarian, the late James Herriot, recorded a tender conversation with a bed-ridden, dying invalid named Miss Stubbs, whose three old dogs and two cats were under his care. After assuring Herriot that she was not afraid to die ("I know there's something better waiting for me. I've never had any doubts."), she opened her heart to a concern millions of pet owners share. "I have only one fear," she explained:

> "It's the dogs and cats, Mr. Herriot. I'm afraid I might never see them when I'm gone which worries me so. You see, I know I'll be reunited with my parents and brothers, but . . .but . . ." She gazed at the two cats curled up at the end of her bed.
>
> "Well, why not with your animals?"
>
> "That's just it." She rocked her head on the pillow and for the first time I saw tears on her cheeks. "They say animals have no souls."
>
> "Who says?"
>
> "Oh, I've read it and I know a lot of religious people believe it."
>
> "Well, I don't believe it." I patted the hand which still grasped mine. "If having a soul means being able to feel

love and loyalty and gratitude, then animals are better off than a lot of humans. You've nothing to worry about there."

"Oh, I hope you're right. Sometimes I lie at night thinking about it."

"I know I'm right, Miss Stubbs, and don't you argue with me. They teach us vets all about animals' souls."

The tension left her face and she laughed with a return of her old spirit. "I'm sorry to bore you with this and I'm not going to talk about it again. But before you go, I want you to be absolutely honest with me. I don't want reassurance from you—just the truth. I know you are very young but please tell me—what are your beliefs? Will my animals go with me?"

She stared intently into my eyes. I shifted my chair and swallowed once or twice.

"Miss Stubbs, I'm afraid I'm a bit foggy about all this," I said. "But I'm absolutely certain of one thing. Wherever you are going, they are going too."

She still stared at me but her face was calm again. "Thank you, Mr. Herriot, I know you are being honest with me. That is what you really believe, isn't it?"

"I do believe it," I said. "With all my heart I believe it."[1]

Miss Stubbs was correct in her observation that "a lot of religious people" believe that animals do not have souls. Generally, there are two reasons for this assumption. Some Christians reject the idea that animals possess souls because the Bible allegedly only speaks about people going to Heaven. It doesn't provide straightforward information on the eternal destiny of animals—so it's assumed they do not possess souls. Other Christians acknowledge that animals *do* possess souls, in terms of some kind of animating life force, but assume that God did not intend for animals to survive physical death. Therefore, their souls are extinguished when life ends.

I reject both views. Although the Bible does not deal explicitly with this issue, I believe a compelling biblical case can be made that animals not only possess souls, but also that their souls will continue to exist after physical death. Human souls are not immortal in and of themselves; only God is eternal and therefore immortal (1 Tim. 6:16). But God has given humans immortal souls. In this chapter, I'll demonstrate that there are good reasons to believe He has also given immortal souls to (at least) sentient animals.

What the Bible Says

That the human soul is immaterial and distinct from our physical bodies is obvious in Scripture. In Matthew 10:28, Jesus warned us not to "be afraid of those who kill the body [*soma*] but cannot kill the soul [*psyche*]." In this passage, as J. P. Moreland points out, "*psyche* seems clearly to refer to something that can exist without the body"[2] (cf. Rev. 6:9). Likewise, in Luke 8:55, when Jesus brought back to life a dead child, the text says that "her spirit returned." This clearly refers to the immaterial dimension of her being—and that it's capable of existing independent of her physical body. We see a similar example of a soul departing a body at death in the Old Testament: "It came about as her [Rachel's] soul was departing (for she died), that she named him Ben-oni; but his father called him Benjamin" (Gen. 35:18; NASB).

However, theological studies on whether or not animals have souls, especially *immortal* souls, have not been high on the church's agenda. Nevertheless, theologians who have commented on the subject seem to agree that animals *do* have souls. Gary Habermas and J.P Moreland point out that "throughout the history of the church, the classic understanding of living things has included the doctrine that animals, as well as humans, have souls. Christians have maintained this because the Bible teaches that animals have souls."[3] Even Christian theologians who are unconvinced that earth-bound animals will inhabit Heaven still recognize the reality of animal souls. Acknowledging that both humans and animals have souls, but denying animal immortality, hunting and trapping advocate Professor Stephen Vantassel writes: "Nor does a semantic review of *nephesh* (soul) provide any support for ontologically separating humans from animals, because both animals and humans share in *nephesh*."[4]

Many theologians down through the ages have believed that animal souls are different from human souls in that animal souls are not immortal. In the thirteenth century, for example, Thomas Aquinas taught that animals were not rational creatures, and, therefore, their souls were no more than an "animating principle" directly associated with their physical bodies. At death, animal souls perish. Human souls, on the other hand, are rational and therefore survive physical death.[5] I'm not sure how Aquinas connects rationality with the existence of immortal souls, but that was his position. With today's growing body of evidence that sentient animals have far greater cognitive abilities than was known in Aquinas' day, I would not be surprised—if Aquinas were alive today—that he would think differently about the immortality of animal souls.

Be this as it may, even today the crux of the argument is not whether animals have souls but whether their souls are immortal. Habermas and Moreland further point out, "Even though the church has been quite clear about the existence of animal souls, there has been no consensus about the existence of animals in the afterlife, some Christians favoring the idea, some arguing against it, some remaining agnostic."[6]

Whether or not animals have *immortal* souls hinges on what the Bible has to say on the topic. This in turn hinges, to a large degree, on the definition and application of two Hebrew words translated in the Old Testament as "soul" and "spirit."

Soul Versus Spirit

Before we examine these two Hebrew words, something should be said about the disagreement among Christians on whether "soul" and "spirit" are synonymous or whether they are two distinct components of a human's immaterial dimension. Some take the position that in the Bible the words for soul and spirit are used interchangeably, and therefore people are comprised of two parts: body and soul/spirit. There is biblical justification for this view, which is called *bipartite*. For example, in John 12:27 Jesus said, "My soul has become troubled;" while in John 13:21 "He became troubled in spirit" (see also Gen. 41:8; Ps. 42:6; Matt. 27:50; Heb.12:23; Rev. 6:9—NASB). In these cases, spirit and soul seem to be used interchangeably.

Other Christians are *tripartite* and believe the Bible teaches that people are composed of three distinct parts: body, soul, *and* spirit. These people view the body as the physical part of our being; the soul is associated with the immaterial "mind" (the seat of emotions, cognition, and will); and the spirit as that part of our being that relates specifically to the spiritual realm, in particular a Christian's personal connectedness with God (e.g. Ps. 51:10; Rom. 8:16).[7] In support of the tripartite view, the Bible sometimes uses soul and spirit in the same verse, implying a clear distinction. For example, Job 7:11 says, "Therefore I will not keep silent; I will speak out in the anguish of my spirit [*ruach*], I will complain in the bitterness of my soul [*nephesh*]." The New Testament makes it even clearer. The Apostle Paul wrote in 1 Thessalonians 5:23, "May your whole spirit [*pneuma*], soul [*psyche*] and body [*soma*] be kept blameless at the coming of our Lord Jesus Christ." Likewise the author of Hebrews wrote, "The word of God is living and active. Sharper than any double-edged sword, it penetrates even to dividing soul [*psyche*] and spirit [*pneuma*]" (4:12).

In favor of the tripartite view, Greek scholar Spiros Zodhiates explains that the New Testament Greek word *pneuma* is distinct from *psyche* in that it represents people's "immaterial nature which enables [them] to communicate with God, who is also spirit," while *psyche* (soul) is the "immaterial part of man held in common with animals."[8]

The question is if human souls are eternal, why wouldn't animal souls be eternal? I believe they are. If the same Greek word for soul is used for both humans and animals—and God gave human souls immortality—it seems reasonable that He may give immortality to animal souls as well. If so, they too will survive physical death. In support of this, the Hebrew words for soul (*nephesh*) *and* spirit (*ruach*) are both applied to animals as well as humans, as we'll see below.

In this study, however, I choose to use just the word "soul," rather than "soul" *and* "spirit," to describe an animal's immaterial dimension. This avoids the risk of implying that animals have a "spirit" in the tripartite sense of a special connectedness with God, which only humans enjoy. I find no biblical evidence that animals have a spirit distinct from their souls. Thus, in the case of animals, the bipartite view is correct. (I personally endorse the tripartite view for humans.) With this said, we can now examine the Hebrew words for soul and spirit and see how they apply to nonhuman life.

Word Study

The initial step for determining whether or not animals have *immortal* souls is to analyze the meaning of the two Hebrew words, *nephesh* and *ruach*. This is not the only biblical evidence we'll examine, but it is the first step. The task at hand, then, is to flesh out the meaning of these two words within the *context* of how they are used in passages relating to animals. If *nephesh* and *ruach* are used to describe human souls and spirits—which we know are immortal—and the same words refer to animal *souls*, it suggests they too may be immortal.

*Nephesh***:** The Hebrew word *nephesh* is translated *soul* 238 times—more than a hundred times its second most common usage (*life*). *Nephesh,* when translated as "soul," refers to our immaterial self—that part of our being that continues to exist once it is released from our bodies at physical death. Moreover, as professor Steve W. Lemke points out, the word is used for both humans and animals: "Scripture uses the same word to describe the animating force that God gave animals (*nephesh,* Gn 1:20-21, 24, 30) as it does in describing how He breathed a living soul into persons (Gn 2:7)."[9] Does this mean the word *nephesh* denotes souls in animals? The following passages suggest it does.[10]

Genesis 1:20: "Let the waters team with swarms of living *creatures*" [*nephesh*].
Genesis 1:24: "Then God said, 'Let the earth bring forth living *creatures* [*nephesh*] after their kind . . .'"
Genesis 1:30: ". . . and to every beast of the earth and to every bird of the sky and to everything that moves on the earth which has *life*" [*nephesh*].
Genesis 2:19: ". . . and whatever [Adam] called a living *creature* [*nephesh*] that was its name."
Job 12:10: "In whose [God's] hand is the life [*nephesh*] of every living thing . . ."
Proverbs 12:10: "The righteous man has regard for the *life* [*nephesh*] of his animal."

Some may argue that in the above passages soul is referring only to an animating "life force," not an *immortal* soul. In the following passages, however, *spirit* is also applied to animals. So even if soul (*nephesh)* means only an animating life force, the fact that spirit (*ruach*) is also applied to animals still implies immortality for animals in the bipartite sense—given that soul and spirit are synonymous in animals. The following passages illustrate this. (As stressed earlier, this does not mean animals possess spirits in the tripartite sense of a special connectedness with God, which only humans enjoy.)

Ruach: The Hebrew word *ruach* is translated breath, wind, or spirit. However, it's used 203 times for *spirit*—more than its usage for breath and wind combined. In the following passages, where *ruach* is translated "breath" rather than "spirit," it can still imply *spirit* when the contexts are speaking of the immaterial essence of both humans *and* animals—as it explicitly does in some of the passages. Thus, the Hebrew word translated *spirit*, just like the Hebrew word translated *soul*, is ascribed to animals:[11]

Genesis 6:17: "Behold, I, even I am bringing the flood of waters upon the earth, to destroy all flesh [human and animal] in which is the *breath* [*ruach*] of life."
Genesis 7:15: "So they went into the ark to Noah, by twos of all flesh in which there was the breath [*ruach*] of life."
Genesis 7:22: ". . . of all that was on the dry land, all in which nostrils was the breath of the *spirit* [*ruach*] of life, died."
Psalm 104: 29: "You hide Your face, they [the animals] are dismayed; You take away their *spirit* [*ruach*] they expire and return to their dust."
Ecclesiastes 3:19: "For the fate of the sons of men and the fate of beasts is the same. As one dies, so dies the other; indeed, they all have the same *breath* [*ruach*] and there is no advantage for man over beast."

This brief word study shows that the Hebrew words translated soul and spirit are applied to both humans and animals. In light of this, if human souls are immortal, it seems reasonable and probable that animal souls are also immortal—especially since nothing in the Bible tells us that animal souls are extinguished upon physical death. Some skeptics, however, disagree. There are three Bible passages they frequently quote to support their assumption that animals do not possess eternal souls. As we examine them, notice that none actually speak to the issue of animal souls.

Scripture Objections Overruled
Psalm 49:10-20

The first is Psalm 49:10-20, in particular verses 15 and 20: "But God will redeem my life from the grave; he will surely take me to himself. . . . A man who has riches without understanding is like the beast that perishes." At first glance—and by ignoring the other verses in the passage—this passage may seem to imply that godly men will be rescued from the grave (resurrected), but animals will perish. Why this interpretation? Because skeptics *assume* the passage is focusing on *spiritual* death. Thus, since animals supposedly lack eternal souls, at death they "decay in the grave" (14) while humans, who do have eternal souls, eventually rise from the grave. But is this what the passage is concerned about? Not at all. Yes, the godly man will "be rescued from the grave," but in context the focus of the passage is that both humans and animals die *physically* (10-12); at death the fate of our bodies is no different than theirs—we all return to dust. The passage is saying nothing about the eternal state of animals. Rather, it's emphasizing the fate of a godless rich man (represented as sheep—v. 14) who "will take nothing with him when he dies" (17). In other words, just as animals have no material possessions to carry to the grave, neither do humans. When people die, regardless of the riches they enjoyed in this life, they take nothing with them to the grave—just like animals. The passage is not about the eternal destiny of animals.

Matthew 25:31-46

The second passage skeptics believe refutes the notion of animals possessing eternal souls is Matthew 25:31-46, especially verse 46:

"Then they [the goats] will go away to eternal punishment, but the righteous to eternal life." But read the entire passage. It's not talking about animals at all. Jesus is distinguishing saved people (represented by the sheep on His right) from unsaved people (the goats on His left—v. 32). The passage is saying nothing whatsoever about whether or not animals (i.e. the sheep and goats) possess souls. Indeed, if it *were* speaking about the destiny of animal souls, at least some (the sheep) *would* "go away . . . to eternal life" (v. 46)!

Ecclesiastes 3:19-21

Probably the most common passage used to discredit the immortality of animal souls is Ecclesiastes 3:19-21:

> For the fate of the sons of men and the fate of beasts is the same. As one dies, so dies the other; indeed, they all have the same breath (*ruach*—spirit) and there is no advantage for man over beast, for all is vanity. All go to the same place. All came from the dust and all return to the dust [i.e. their physical bodies]. Who knows that the breath (*ruach*—spirit) of the beast descends downward to the earth?"

Skeptics of animal immortality interpret this passage to mean that while the bodies of people and animals both decay (turn to dust), human immortal spirits go to Heaven but animal spirits do not. Again, this is an assumption. The author points out that human and animal bodies "all go to the same place." Then he *asks a question* (not make a statement): "Who knows" if the breath (i.e. *ruach*—spirit) of animals "descends downward to the earth?" The most obvious interpretation of this passage would be the *opposite* of the skeptic's. If the "fate" of human and animal bodies is the same, that is, "all go to the same place," the author may well have assumed that human and animal spirits also go to the same place.

But perhaps he wasn't absolutely certain about it (just like many Christians), so he asked the question: "Who knows that the breath (*ruach*—spirit) of the beast descends downward to the earth?"

Some skeptics have attempted to support their interpretation by arguing that verse 12:7 clarifies the issue. When the teacher says, "and the dust returns to the ground it came from, and the spirit returns to God who gave it," they *assume* that the dust returning to the ground is the animal's spirit in verse 3:21. Thus, animal spirits are extinguished at death while human spirits ascend to God. This is pure speculation. In context of all of chapter twelve, verse 12:7 is obviously referring just to people. It's saying that people's spirits go to God while their physical bodies return to dust. It says nothing about animal spirits.

As these three examples illustrate, the passages skeptics rely on to justify their belief that animals do not possess immortal souls, in reality, say no such thing. To conclude otherwise requires the skeptic to read his or her own presumptions *back into the text.*

Still, this alone may not convince some skeptics that animals possess *immortal* souls. They typically raise several other objections. As we examine them, it's important to note that there is a logical flaw in all of them. Every argument put forward to deny the existence of immortal animal souls are *assumptions*, that is, all of them *presuppose*—without biblical justification—that animal souls are extinguished at physical death, when in fact nowhere does the Bible make such a claim.

Other Objections Overruled
Animals Lack the Qualifying Mental Attributes That Indicate the Presence of an Immortal Soul

This argument claims that animals do not have immortal souls because they lack soul-like qualities; that is, the cognitive and emotional attributes that humans associate with the existence of an immaterial mind, which we saw is the essential faculty of an immortal soul. This argument was laid to rest in chapter three, but let me add this.

Even if animals do not possess human-like thoughts and emotions and functioned instead on mere instinct, there is still no reason why God would not grant them eternal souls and extend His love for them into the next life. He may do so for no other reason than His own pleasure—and the pleasure they will give humans. On this Earth, wildlife is what makes the wilderness enjoyably wild, and numerous varieties of animals are our friends and companions. Nothing in Scripture suggests that the restored New Earth will be inhabited only by redeemed humans, or that animals will not continue their present earthly roles in Heaven. Indeed, the Old Testament in particular says much about animals in God's eternal Kingdom—as we'll see in chapter seven.

Even if God did create animals only to have instrumental value for humans, as some skeptics believe, there is *still* no reason why the animals that serve and bless humanity in this life would not continue to serve and bless us as friends and companions in Heaven. I like the way Randy Alcorn put it:

> Why [do] so many people find such companionship, solace, and joy in their pets?. . . I believe it's because of how God has made animals, and us. . . . It would be simple for him to re-create a pet in Heaven if he wants to. He's the *giver* of all good gifts, not the *taker* of them. If it would please us to have a pet restored to the New Earth, that may be sufficient reason" (emphasis included).[12]

Human Dominion over Animals Means They Do Not Have Souls
This argument claims that because the human race was instructed to have "dominion" over the animal kingdom (Gen. 1:28, KJV),

animals do not possess immortal souls. This is probably the weakest argument against animal immortality. Not only is it clearly a *non sequitur*, it makes no theological sense. On the contrary, God's instruction for the human race to have dominion ("rule" in newer translations) over the animal kingdom is actually evidence that animals *do* possess immortal souls.

In order to see this, it requires an understanding of what human dominion over animals means within a biblical framework. It *doesn't* mean that humans are given full authority to use and exploit nonhuman life with no regard for their welfare. Most theologians agree that dominion means *stewardship*. It denotes mankind's caretaker role in creation. Dominion doesn't give people a license to use animals anyway they please; it's managing God's property (Ps. 50:10-11) in a way that conforms to His love and provision for all creation, including animals.

God designed Earth to support animals as well as people, and He assigned to the human race, beginning with Adam, the responsibility to be His custodians or managers over *all* creation, including animals. We are obligated, therefore, to see that threatened and endangered animals are protected, to set aside and protect natural habitats vital for wildlife, to humanely care for domesticated animals, and so on.

I have explored this topic fully elsewhere, and space prevents a recapitulation here.[13] But let me say again, as we saw in chapter one, that God loves, enjoys, provides for, and values the creatures He created. If human dominion (stewardship) over animals teaches us anything, it's that God wants His overseers (the human race) to protect wildlife from destructive exploitation and abuse, thereby allowing them to pursue the purposes for which He created them. Would God give us this responsibility if His love for nonhuman life ended with their physical death? It seems much more reasonable, because of His love and joy for the animals inhabiting Earth today, that God will extend their existence into eternity. I believe

God has more in mind for animals than their short sojourn on this present Earth.[14]

Only Humans Were Created in God's Image—Thus Animals Do Not Have Immortal Souls

This is probably the most common argument used as proof that animals are merely physical creatures without immortal souls. The assumption is that because only humans were created in God's image, animal souls expire at physical death.

It's unarguable that humans have a special relationship with God that animals do not share. We are the crown of God's creation (Ps. 8:4-8), and of far greater value to Him than animals (Matt. 6:26). And as we saw previously, animals have souls but not spirits. Thus, they do not have the spiritual connectedness with God that humans enjoy by virtue of our creation in His image (Gen. 1:27). As such, humans alone possess the *communicable* attributes of God and therefore are able to understand and discern the things of God (1 Cor. 2:10-13). Furthermore, as far as anyone can tell, at least on this present Earth, only humans are innately aware that God exists (Eccl. 3:11; Rom.1:19-20).

But why does this mean that animals can't have immortal souls? It doesn't. God could bless animals with immortal souls if He chooses to do so, and it's presumptuous to say He can't. Theologian Andrew Linzey sums it up well:

There is something theologically odd about all discussions of immortal souls—the plain absurdity, no less, of humans deciding for themselves which essential or substantial qualities qualify them for eternal life and which may or may not exclude animals. . . . Eternal life is God's own gift; it is not something which we can merit. . . . If full weight is given to

God's gracious and wide-ranging activity in creation, then it is inconceivable that the God who redeems will be *less* than the God who creates. In this sense the issue of animal immortality is wholly integral to the view that God does actually care not only for the whole world but for each and every individual being within it, including—of course—sparrows.[15]

The Major Reason Some People Reject Animal Immortality

Let me summarize this chapter by making a few final comments on why I think so many people reject the idea of animal immortality. It's true that animals do not possess spirits in the *tripartite* sense of a unique spiritual connection with God, which only humans enjoy by virtue of being created in His image. But this is no reason to conclude that animal souls are merely corporeal and without God-given eternal qualities. The fact is, nothing in Scripture speaks about the annihilation of animal souls at physical death. Thus, if animals do have souls, it seems reasonable and probable they would be gifted with *immortal* souls—just like humans.

I believe the major reason many people reject animal immortality is not for biblical reasons at all—but for emotional reasons. They worry that if we admit animal souls are eternal, we are either elevating animals to human status or are acquiescing to some kind of pagan, earth-based religion where there is no value distinction between people and animals. There is no reason to have this concern. Animals were not created the same as humans (1 Cor. 15:39), nor do animals have the same value to God as people (Matt. 6:26). In the future New Earth, we can expect these distinctions to remain. (We'll look at this in detail later.) Just because animals have souls that survive physical death does not change their status in the here-and-now nor in the age to come. Animals in Heaven will still be just animals.

I believe the biblical evidence presented in this chapter sufficiently demonstrates that God has not only blessed animals with souls, but with immortal souls. The arguments skeptics muster to refute this are unsustainable and without biblical justification. They *assume* that animals don't have immortal souls—but can offer no objective biblical evidence or legitimate arguments to support it.

If God gave animals immortal souls, the question that follows on the heels of this is whether or not their souls will one day be reunited with their physical bodies. In other words, in the future new heaven and earth, will animals be *resurrected* alongside redeemed humans? I believe they will, and I'll systematically develop evidence to support this in chapter eight. Before I do this, however, I need to lay a biblical foundation on which evidence for animal resurrection will rest. This will entail establishing continuity between this Earth and the prophesied new heaven and earth revealed in both the Old and New Testaments. This will be the focus of part two.

Part Two

People, Pets, and Wildlife in the New Heaven and Earth

CHAPTER 5

Where Will the Prophesied Eternal Home of God's People and Animals Be Located?

The pleasant feelings we all seem to have when we
are trusted by wild animals may be an indication
that in the heart of every person is a longing for
the harmony that once reigned in the Garden of
Eden. In fact, the Bible describes not only that
lost paradise, but also a future paradise.

DEAN OHLMAN[1]

From beginning to end, the Bible recounts the ongoing story of creation and redemption. Genesis chapters one and two tell us what God did in the beginning. The Psalmists proclaim the beauty and wonder of creation. Jesus prayed for the Father's kingdom to come and that His will "be done on earth as it is in heaven" (Matt. 6: 10). He said that the "poor in spirit" would inherit the "kingdom of *heaven*" and the "meek" would inherit the *earth* (Matt. 5:3, 5, emphasis added), likely referring to the future "new heaven and earth" (Rev. 21:1). In terms of the eschaton, the Old Testament prophets and Revelation tell us what God will do at the end of this present age. In particular, creation will be redeemed, transformed, and *united* with Heaven. The merging of these two realities—the physical with the spiritual—will become literally Heaven on Earth; the everlasting abode of God's people and animals.

This and the following chapter may seem to drift away from the focus of this book, which is to demonstrate that pets and other animal will inhabit Heaven, along with God's people. But there is a reason for this relevant detour. The best way to envision why soul-bearing, earth-bound animals will inhabit Heaven is to see that there is *continuity* between Earth, its human and animal inhabitants, and the new heaven and earth prophesied in the Old and New Testaments. In other words, if *this* Earth is going to be the locus of the future new heaven and earth, it's a compelling reason to believe that animals inhabiting Earth today will be the same kinds of animals that will inhabit Heaven.

Where will the redeemed and restored new heaven and earth be located, which Isaiah (65:17; 66:22), Peter (2 Pet. 3:13), John (Rev. 21:1), and others prophesied? And why is this important in order to demonstrate that at least sentient animals will inhabit this eternal abode? This is the subject of the present chapter.

Heaven on Earth

The Bible refers to the future eternal home of redeemed and resurrected humans—those who are saved by the atoning work of Jesus Christ (1 Cor. 15:3; 2 Cor. 5:21)—as a *new heaven and a new earth* (Rev. 21:1-4). The *Evangelical Dictionary of Theology* describes it this way:

> The biblical doctrine of the created universe includes the certainty of its final redemption from the dominion of sin. The finally redeemed universe is called "the new heavens and new earth" . . .
>
> The new heavens and the new earth will be the renewed creation that will fulfill the purpose for which God created

the universe. It will be characterized by the complete rule of God and by the full realization of the final goal of redemption: "Behold the dwelling of God is with men" (Rev. 21:3).[2]

This bare-bones description gives us the theological *fact* of the new heaven and earth, but not what it's like or where it will be located. It does, however, reveal the two most important features of this prophesied "redeemed universe" and "renewed creation:" Sin will be permanently vanquished and God will dwell with His people forever. But this doctrinal statement omits any description of the physical environment of the new heaven and earth or its animal inhabitants. There are passages in the Bible that do, however, and we'll look at many of them as we move through the following two chapters. But my focus for now is on where this *New Earth* (i.e. Heaven) will be located. Again, this is important in order to confirm that there will be continuity between our present Earth and the future new heaven and earth—and its animal inhabitants.

The first thing that needs to be established is that Heaven is *not* an alien, mysterious, otherworldly place located somewhere "far off in space." Rather, Heaven will actually encompass *this* Earth, but transformed and restored (hence the term *New Earth*—Rev. 21:1-4). To be sure, the wicked will be take away from Earth (Rev. 20:7-15) and the righteous will inherit it (Rev. 5:10; cf. Matt. 5:5). But nothing in Old or New Testament eschatology suggests that God's children will be removed from Earth and transported to some kind of parallel universe or to a Heaven located far out in the cosmos. Hank Hanegraaff, president of the Christian Research Institute, puts it plainly,

> The grand and glorious promise of the biblical worldview is that we will once again walk this physical planet. . . .
> You and I are not going anywhere! Heaven and earth [will be] conjoined. . . . When [Jesus] appears again heaven

and earth will be as one—united, as it was before the advent of decay, disease, destruction, and death. The dwelling of God will be here. . . .

We are not going to be resurrected to another world. We await our resurrection in this world! This world is not about to be scrapped; it will ultimately be redeemed.[3]

Now, this needs some elaboration. When we Christians die, our *souls* go immediately to be with the Lord in Heaven (2 Cor. 5:1-8; Phil 1:21-23). At the end of this age, when Jesus returns to initiate His eternal Kingdom, our souls will then be reunited with our resurrected bodies (1 Cor. 15; Phil. 3:21). At that point, Heaven will unite with the redeemed and transformed *New* Earth to become our flawless, eternal home—one free forever of sin, suffering, grief, hardships, natural disasters, and all the others evils that plague the human race and nature on Earth today. Here's how this plays out in the eschaton.

Heaven Will Include the New Earth

The Bible reveals that at the end of this age, when Jesus returns, Earth will be redeemed and transformed into a New Earth. In other words, as emphasized, there will be continuity between *this Earth* and the restored New Earth. The prophet Ezekiel gives an example of this continuity when he spoke of Israel's restoration in the prophesied Messianic Age. He wrote that a river will flow "east through the desert into the valley of the Dead Sea. The waters of this stream will make the salty waters of the Dead Sea fresh and pure. . . . Fish will abound in the Dead Sea, for its waters will become fresh" (47:8–9 NLT). Unless God creates another Dead Sea on another earth, this prophecy will be fulfilled here on Earth.

One of the most significant New Testament prophesies revealing the continuity between the old and new Earth is Revelation

21:2-27. This passage describes a prophesied *new Jerusalem* (also Rev. 3:12; cf. Isa. 65:17-19) descending onto Earth when Jesus returns to establish His eternal Kingdom (Rev. 19:11- 20:15). Both the Old and New Testaments juxtapose this Holy City with a restored creation (see Isa. 65: 17- 25; Rev. 21:1-2; 22:1-5; cf. Rom. 8:19-23). Distinguished professor of Old Testament at Denver Seminary, M. Daniel Carroll R., gives us a thrilling glimpse into what the harmonious co-existence of the Holy City with nature may be like:

> To this glorious city and surrounding rural areas is added a picture of tranquility in nature (Is 65:25). . . . The important point to grasp is the conjunction between the chief urban center in the Bible (Jerusalem) and a bountiful and peaceful creation (cf. Mic. 4:1-4). This hope of wedding human habitations to the marvels of creation is the goal to which God is sovereignly moving history. Harmony between humankind and the created order finally will be restored. Nevertheless, this is not a return to the Eden, to a pristine garden without the footprints of civilization. This is another kind of paradise, one with both cities and farms.[4]

There is disagreement on whether this Holy City is an actual city descending onto Earth (Rev. 21:2, 10), or a symbolic representation of the perfected eternal Church, the body of Christ (Heb.12:22). However, with so much detailed description of the new Jerusalem in Revelation, it seems likely that it is a literal city (Rev. 21:10-17).

Either way, the new Jerusalem descending onto Earth, says the late theologian Anthony Hoekema, marks "the final state, heaven and earth will have merged!" Hoekema explains:

> The "new Jerusalem" stands for the entire glorified church of God. This church . . . does not remain in a "heaven"

far off in space, but it comes down to the renewed earth; there [the] redeemed will spend eternity in resurrection bodies. So heaven and earth, now separated, will then be merged: the new earth will also be heaven, since God will dwell there with his people. Glorified believers, in other words, will continue to be in heaven while they are inhabiting the new earth.[5]

The Earth Will Be Redeemed and Purified—Not Destroyed

During a radio interview shortly after my book *Should Christians Be Environmentalists?* was released, the host put forward a common argument some Christians use to justify unnecessary environmental exploitation: "Why should we care what happens to the environment if God is going to destroy Earth at the end of this age?"[6] This argument is based on 2 Peter 3:10-13, which reads in part,

> But the day of the Lord will come like a thief. The heavens will disappear with a roar; the elements will be destroyed by fire, and the earth and everything in it will be laid bare. . . . But in keeping with his promise we are looking forward to a new heaven and a new earth, the home of righteousness (10, 13).

This passage *appears* to say that there will be a fiery cataclysmic end to Earth, perhaps by nuclear war, a collision between Earth and an asteroid or comet, or some other cosmic event that will totally annihilate the planet. This will happen on "the day of the Lord" (v. 10), when Jesus returns to crush Satan and his minions and then recreate a "new" heaven and earth (Rev. 20-22).

I don't agree with this interpretation for several reasons. For one, it's the only passage in the Bible, which I'm aware of, that seems to imply Earth will be destroyed by fire at the end of this age. Instead, the Bible teaches that following judgment, Earth will be redeemed and restored not annihilated. Numerous passages in both the Old and New Testaments confirm this. The following are a few examples.

(Note: In the following passages "heaven" refers to the atmosphere above the earth and outer space. The only exception is Acts 3:21, where "heaven" refers to the dwelling place of God, angels, and saved humanity.)

The Earth Will "Perish . . . Wear out . . . Change . . . [Be] Discarded . . . Pass Away"

Psalm 102:25-26

"In the beginning you [God] laid the foundations of the earth, and the heavens are the work of your hands. They will perish, but you remain; they will all wear out like a garment. Like clothing you will change them and they will be discarded."

Isaiah 51:6

"Lift up your eyes to the heavens, look at the earth beneath; the heavens will vanish like smoke, the earth will wear out like a garment and its inhabitants die like flies. But my salvation will last forever, my righteousness will never fail."

Matthew 24:35

[Jesus said,] "heaven and earth will pass away, but my words will never pass away."

Hebrews 1:10-12

"In the beginning, O' Lord, you laid the foundations of the earth, and the heavens are the work of your hands. They will perish, but you remain; they will all wear out like a garment. You will roll them up like a robe; like a garment they will be changed."

There Will Be a New Earth

Just as there are passages that reveal the present heaven and earth will pass away, there are also Old and New Testament passages that predict a *new* heaven and earth.

Isaiah 65:17

"Behold, I [God] will create new heavens and a new earth. The former things will not be remembered, nor will they come to mind."

Isaiah 66:22

"As the new heavens and the new earth that I make will endure before me," declares the LORD, "so will your name and descendants endure."

Acts 3:21

"He [Jesus] must remain in heaven [where God dwells] until the time comes for God to *restore* everything, as he promised long ago through his holy prophets (emphasis added)."

Revelation 21:1

"Then I saw a new heaven and a new earth, for the first heaven and the first earth had passed away. . ."

None of the passages quoted require an interpretation that Earth will be destroyed by fire (or in any other way) in the eschaton. Isaiah 51:6 and Hebrews 1:11 say Earth will "wear out." The other passages say (or add) that Earth will "perish," "change," or "pass away." On the other hand, there are passages that clearly state Earth *will* remain forever. Here are a few examples:

Psalm 78:69

"He [God] built his sanctuary like the heights, like the earth that he established forever."

Psalm 104:5

"He set the earth on its foundation; it can never be moved."

Ecclesiastes 1:4

"Generations come and generations go, but the earth remains forever."

Revelation 5:10

"You made them [redeemed people] to be a kingdom and priests to serve our God, and they will reign on the earth [in the eschaton]."

It should also be pointed out that fire is often associated with judgment in the Bible (e.g. Ps. 97:3; 1 Cor. 3:15). So rather than a fire *literally* destroying Earth, and God creating a brand new Earth from scratch, Peter is likely speaking about Earth being judged, redeemed, and purified. Moreover, the Greek word for "new" in 2 Peter 3:13 is *Kainós*, which "refers to [a] heaven and earth which have been renewed, and, therefore, made superior, more splendid; as also the 'new Jerusalem' (Rev. 3:12; 21:2)."[7]

And finally, in Genesis 8:21 God promised He would never again "curse the ground because of man" or "destroy all living creatures" as He did in the Noahic Flood. This promise would seem to contradict 2 Peter 3:10-13 *if* Earth was literally destroyed by fire prior to the restoration and renewal of nature. Again, this is in harmony with the interpretation that Peter is speaking of judgment, not literal annihilation by fire.

What the Bible Actually Says about the Transformation of the Present Earth into the New Earth.

A more accurate exegesis of 2 Peter 3:10-13 suggests that the interpretation of Earth being literally destroyed by fire ("burned-up" in some translations) is incorrect. Rather, the text actually carries the idea that Earth will be "laid bare" (NIV), that is, purged of sin and evil as a prelude to a restored and redeemed creation on *this* Earth. "The Greek word for 'destroy' in 2 Peter 3:10-12," writes Douglas Moo, professor of New Testament at Wheaton College, "is a verb that denotes . . . 'to destroy or reduce something to ruin by tearing down or breaking to pieces' . . . Most scholars correctly resist the conclusion that this language points to the doctrine of annihilationism."[8]

Steven Bouma-Prediger, professor of religion at Hope College agrees:

To put it bluntly, this verse [2 Pet. 3:10] represents perhaps the most egregious mistranslation in the entire New Testament. . . . The [Greek] text states that after a refiner's fire of purification (v. 7), the new earth will be *found*, not burned up. The earth will be *discovered*, not destroyed. . . . [The text] refers, rather, to the purification and renewal of creation. As [Christian scholar] Thomas Finger insists in his careful study of this text, "The main emphasis of the text is that everything will be scrutinized or assessed by God, and not necessarily destroyed." Thus, 2 Peter 3 rightly rendered speaks of a basic continuity rather than discontinuity of this world with the next.[9]

Reformation theologian John Calvin supported this position. Susan Schreiner, a recognized authority on John Calvin, writes

Calvin argued that there is a fundamental, unbroken continuity of creation, a restoration of order in the world, and a reestablishment of the revelatory function of nature. . . .

[T]he cosmos will be purified but not destroyed. . . . Calvin contended that God will not abandon creation; instead, God will renovate its original material. . . .

Therefore, in Calvin's view, the fires of judgment will not destroy creation but will purify its original and enduring substance. With this argument, Calvin portrayed God as faithful to his original creation. Just as God brought the cosmos into being, closely governs and restrains its natural forces, so too he will renew and transform its original substance.[10]

There is a fundamental principle of biblical hermeneutics (interpretation) that applies here. This basic rule is that we always interpret a passage of Scripture within context of surrounding passages as well as within context of other passages that speak on the same topic. With regard to 2 Peter 3:10, every other passage in the Old and New Testaments that speaks about the new heaven and earth say nothing about the present Earth being destroyed by fire. The angel proclaims in Revelation 11:15, "The kingdom of the world has become the kingdom of our Lord and of His Christ, and he will reign for ever and ever." He doesn't say the kingdom of the world will be destroyed. Jesus didn't come to destroy the world and its inhabitants but to save it (John 3:16) and to redeem the earth (Rom. 8:19-23). Revelation 5:9-10 teaches that people "purchased" by Jesus' blood would include "every tribe and language and people and nation . . . and they will reign on the *earth*" (emphasis added).

When read in context and alongside other passages referring to the transition of this Earth into the New Earth, it seems clear that 2 Peter 3:10-13 does not mean our planet will be literally, physically destroyed. This can even be established within the context of the passage itself. In verses 3-7, Peter uses the worldwide Flood as an illustration of Earth being "destroyed" (v. 6). But Earth wasn't literally destroyed—it didn't cease to exist. Noah, his family, and at least two of every animal were spared to repopulate Earth after it was judged and cleansed of sin and evil by the flood waters. Obviously, in verse 6, Peter didn't have the total annihilation of Earth in mind. It's unlikely the corresponding "destroyed" in verse 10 would mean utter destruction by fire. Earth will not be obliterated but transformed.

In Acts 3:21 Peter preached that Jesus would "remain in heaven until the time comes for God to restore everything, as he promised long ago through his holy prophets." Destroy and restore mean two entirely different things. Furthermore, the apostle Paul tells us in Colossians 1:19-20 that, through Jesus

Christ, God will "reconcile to himself all things, whether things on earth or things in heaven." He doesn't say God will reconcile all things after He first destroys all things. Jesus Himself refers to "the renewal of all things" when He returns to set up His eternal Kingdom in Matthew 19:28.

In light of these and other passages, it seems certain that in 2 Peter 3:10-13 the apostle is speaking *figuratively* when referring to Earth being destroyed by fire. That is, Peter is speaking about judgment followed by a purified and renewed creation, not annihilation. Earth will be cleansed of evil and creation's curse removed.

Having said this, however, it's important to understand that even if Earth *is* destroyed by fire it doesn't mean the planet will vanish. And it changes nothing with regard to God's eschatological purpose to redeem and decontaminate the earth of sin and to restore it to Garden of Eden-like conditions, as prophesized in Isaiah 51:3 and Ezekiel 36:35. The apostle Paul states this plainly in Romans:

> For all creation is waiting eagerly for that future day when God will reveal who his children really are. Against its will, all creation was subjected to God's curse. But with eager hope, the creation looks forward to the day when it will join God's children in glorious freedom from death and decay. For we know that all creation has been groaning as in the pains of childbirth right up to the present time. And we believers also groan, even though we have the Holy Spirit within us as a foretaste of future glory, for we long for our bodies to be released from sin and suffering. We, too, wait with eager hope for the day when God will give us our full rights as his adopted children, including the new bodies he has promised us (Rom. 8:19-23, NLT).

Paul says nothing in this passage about the destruction of Earth. Nor was he making new end-times revelation. Rather, Paul is supporting what had been proclaimed by the Old Testament prophets for centuries, but through the lens of what would become New Testament fulfillment (see chapter six). In particular, Paul is writing about the removal of the curse and the redemption of all creation (which will include animals) when Jesus returns to establish His everlasting Kingdom. Just as God will transform our mortal bodies into glorious sin-free bodies at the resurrection, rather than create entirely different bodies (Rom. 8:11; 1 Cor.15:35–53; Phil. 3:20-21), so too the first creation will *not* be destroyed and replaced by an entirely new creation; it will be transformed. Earth will be restored and renewed; sin will be obliterated and the curse removed; and humans and animals will coexist in eternal peace (Isa.11:6-9). This is all part of God's redemptive plan for redeemed humanity and restored creation. The prophet Hosea speaks of this eschatological New Earth when he prophesized,

> In that day I [God] will make a covenant for them
>   with the beasts of the field and the birds of
>   the air
>   and the creatures that move along the
>   ground.
> Bow and sword and battle
>   I will abolish from the land,
>   so that all may lie down in safety (2:18).

Why is all this important for the purposes of this particular study? The reason is because the *continuity* between our present Earth and the eschatological New Earth allows features described in Old Testament prophecies about the future new heaven and earth to be literal features in the New Earth. For example, the prophecies in Isaiah 11:6-9 and 65:25, where humans and animals coexist peacefully, are an accurate depiction of the relationship that will exist between humans and animals in transformed nature.

What will this redeem, transformed New Earth be like; this eternal home of God's people and animals? It will be similar to the Garden of Eden—but better! Paradise lost will become paradise regained and glorified. This brings us to the next chapter.

CHAPTER 6

What Will the Eternal Home of God's People and Animals Be Like?

The pure air of heaven filled his lungs. He saw horses and deer and dogs and cats and rabbits and squirrels and badgers and hedgehogs. Until now he'd never thought of animals celebrating or lost in joy, but that's exactly the impression he got when seeing them run and frolic and play with each other and with people. He saw trees that cast light instead of shadows. Some of them hung heavy with citrus fruits, picked and eaten freely by passersby. . . .

The best parts of that other world, he realized, had been but sneak previews of this one. . . .

Compared to what he now beheld, the world he'd come from was a land of shadows, colorless and two-dimensional. This place was fresh and captivating, resonating with color and beauty. He could not only see and hear it, but feel and smell and taste it. Every hillside, every mountain, every waterfall, every frolicking animal in the fields seems to beckon him to come join them, to come from the outside and plunge into the inside. This whole world had the feel of cool water on a blistering August afternoon. The light beckoned him to dive in with abandon, to come join the great adventure[1]

Who would not wish to experience eternity in Heaven as described in Randy Alcorn's novel, *Safely Home*? But is it a realistic portrayal? Will humans run, frolic, and play with horses, deer, dogs, cats, badgers and other wild and domesticated animals? Just how accurate is Alcorn's description of Heaven, when measured against biblical revelation? I believe this chapter will reveal that it's *very* accurate. And I for one look forward to joining the "great adventure" in the age to come.

Before we get started, a couple preliminary things need to be said upfront.

First, the Bible doesn't give us all the information we wish we had with regard to what Heaven will be like. Rather, it's more like the trailer of a movie—a stirring glimpse of what the full feature will reveal; a partial unfolding of the rose, but not the full blossom. As the apostle Paul wrote, "No eye has seen, no ear has heard, no mind has conceived what God has prepared for those who love him" (1 Cor. 2:9). Still, there is enough information about Heaven in Holy Scripture to allow us to draw some legitimate conclusions, which I believe to be sensible and accurate.

Second, some of what I'm about to share from Scripture regarding the prophesied new heaven and earth may be understood differently by some readers. Fair enough. On the other hand, *nothing* I suggest is outside biblical possibilities (I believe probabilities)— or contrary to established, orthodox biblical truths. What follows can be reasonably assumed not only from the Bible but also from what we know of God's great love for all created life (see chapter one).

The New Earth Will Resemble the Garden of Eden

The New Testament does not describe the *natural* environment in the prophesied future New Earth (Heaven). On the other hand, the Old Testament does give tantalizing glimpses of what the physical environment of the New Earth may look like. The Israelites understood that the future kingdom of God would be on *this* Earth; spiritually restored Israel would be an earthly abode. For example, the prophet Ezekiel wrote that on the renewed earth the Dead Sea will be purified with fresh water and inhabited by "swarms of living creatures" (47:8-9). Indeed, the Old Testament prophets foresaw the New Earth as being similar, in many respects, to the Garden of Eden.

Speaking about the prophesized future kingdom of God, Isaiah told the Israelites that "The Lord will surely comfort Zion and will look with compassion on all her ruins; he will make her deserts like Eden, her wastelands like the garden of the Lord. Joy and gladness will be found in her, thanksgiving and the sound of singing" (51:3).

Looking forward to the Israelites return from Babylonian captivity, Ezekiel made a similar prophetic statement. But in context of the entire passage (and other passages in Ezekiel), the prophecy also reflects a messianic hope that will only take place at the end of this present age. He writes, "They [the Israelites] will say, 'This land that was laid waste has become like the garden of Eden'" (36:35).

What did the Garden of Eden look like? Since God was its Creator, it would have been unspoiled, pristine, and indescribably beautiful. There was no death in Eden since it was created before the Fall and nature's subsequent curse (Gen. 2-3). Thus, natural disasters, such as earthquakes, tornadoes, hurricanes, and tsunamis would have been unknown. Furthermore, there could not have been predators or other dangerous animals in Eden, and poisonous and harmful plants would have been absent. Adam and Eve, and all the animal inhabitants of the Garden, were vegetarians (Gen.1:29–30), and food was bountiful and available merely by harvesting it (2:16). Adam and Eve's only responsibility was to tend and care for the Garden (2:15). They didn't even have to water it (2:10). In short, the Garden of Eden was a paradise, a place where humans lived in harmony with other living creatures and in friendship with God.

The Bible further describes the natural environment in which God placed the first couple as having "all kinds of trees . . . that were pleasing to the eye and good for food" (Gen. 2:9). Perhaps these trees resembled the great forests of Lebanon, which God planted (Ps. 104:16). Ezekiel parabolically compares the ancient cedars of Lebanon, whose magnificence was widely proclaimed in the ancient world, with the trees in the Garden of Eden (Ezek. 31:1-9 cf. Isa. 35:1-2). In any case, Eden was probably not a manicured garden in the sense of what we think of as a garden today. (Perhaps it's referred to as a "garden" because God planted it—Genesis 2:8.) Certainly, the Garden of Eden would have included an abundance of flourishing, edible green plants to feed and shelter humans and animals (Gen.1:29-30), as well as wild, stunning, natural forests along with a variety of exotic, colorful vegetation.[2]

Old and New Testament passages that refer to the prophesized future New Earth provide similar parallels with the Garden of Eden. For example, the Holy City (new Jerusalem) that will descend onto Earth from Heaven (Rev. 3:12; 21:10) will have, like Eden, a flowing river and tree of life (cf. Gen. 2:8-10; Rev. 22:1-2). Isaiah declares that the New Earth will have no deserts or wastelands (51:3; cf. 35:1, 7). In chapter eleven Isaiah further reveals that the future Kingdom of God will have no predators or dangerous animals: "The wolf will live with the lamb, the leopard will lie down with the goat, the calf and the lion and the yearling together. . . . The cow will feed with the bear, their young will lie down together . . . and the lion will eat straw like the ox. . . . [T]he young child [will] put his hand into the viper's nest" (6-8). So although wolves, leopards, and lions will inhabit the New Earth, they will no longer be carnivorous or dangerous to humans and each other. In fact carnivores will become herbivores (Isa. 11: 7), and wild nature and humanity will serenely co-exist in this future *Peaceable Kingdom*, as the Isaiah passage is often referred to.

What an amazing and wonderful world to look forward to; a place where *dogs* will no longer chase cats!

Notice that all the prophetic passages I've quoted or referenced, which illustrate parallels between the Garden of Eden and the New Earth (Heaven), were made within an *historical* context that anticipates an eschatological future Kingdom. Even Old Testament passages that seem to focus primarily on the *spiritual* restoration of Israel forecast the future New Earth as an eternal Peaceable Kingdom (see appendix two). We can be certain that an ecological balance, restored habitats, transformed predators, and peaceful relationship between humans and animals will be a *literal* reality on the New Earth.

The New Earth Will *Surpass* the Garden of Eden

Although the Garden of Eden may be its prototype, the future New Earth will be far more magnificent. It will surpass even Eden in grandeur, wonder, splendor, beauty, and enchantment. Referring to the Isaiah eleven passage, Bible scholar and theologian Richard Bauckham put it this way:

> That a new creative act of God is envisaged [by the Old Testament prophets] is certainly right. The new creation surpasses Eden, but one could also say it realizes the potential of Eden. The original innocence of humans and animals does provide the prophet with a model for what the future will be like. It relates the future to what has been God's will for his creatures from the beginning, and it sees that divine intention achieving its goal fully in the future, after which there cannot be another fall into violence.[3]

In terms of its *physical* environment, the New Earth will have many similarities to our present Earth. As Randy Alcorn points out, "The New Earth will not be a non-Earth but a real Earth . . . with dirt, water, rocks, trees, flowers, animals, people, and a variety of natural wonders. An earth without these would not be Earth.[4]

But the eschatological New Earth will be much more than a reinvigorated Garden of Eden. It will be *Heaven* itself! It will have many astonishing features that differ radically from what we experience on Earth today. There will be no seas on the New Earth (Rev. 21:1). Nor will light be derived entirely (if at all) from the sun and moon (Isa. 60:19-20; Rev. 21:23). Unlike Eden, the New Earth will encompass more than nature. There will be civilizations, including nations, rulers, and cultures (Rev. 5:9-10). Indeed, the metaphorical language used to describe the new Jerusalem (precious minerals, pearls, golden streets, etc.— Revelation 21:18-21) indicates a world that humans words cannot adequately describe.

Best of all "there will be no more death or mourning or crying or pain" in the New Earth (Rev. 21:4). Nor will the human population include "the cowardly, the unbelieving, the vile, the murders, the sexually immoral, those who practice magic arts, the idolaters and all liars—their place will be in the fiery lake of burning sulfur" (21:8). In short, there will be no evil or sin or the possibility of a second Fall in the redeemed and restored New Earth (Heaven) because Satan and his minions would have been cast into hell "for ever and ever" (20:10).

But what makes this New Earth truly Heaven—and distinct from the Garden of Eden—is that God will dwell there with His people (Rev. 21:3)! While God visited the Garden of Eden (Gen. 3:8), He will actually reside on the New Earth (Rev. 21:3)! Saved, resurrected humans will see the Lord Jesus Christ face-to-face and live with Him forever (1 Thess. 4:16-18; Rev. 22:3-4).

The Dream That Will Come True

There is another and fascinating reason why we can be certain the New Earth will resemble the Garden of Eden—even surpass it. For some Christian theologians, it is compelling *non-biblical* evidence for the reality of the prophesied new heaven and earth. The human race *intuitively knows* that an eschatological Peaceable Kingdom is a future reality!

I believe a persuasive case can be made that the human race possesses an innate, subconscious memory of the Garden of Eden—and a compelling desire to return. Intrinsic to every human heart is a longing to live in a place of serenity; a place free of evil, suffering, and sorrow; a place where humans, the animal kingdom, and all of nature can coexist in peace. Eden was such a place, and nature provides a glimpse (albeit imperfect) of this home God originally intended for His people—which will again become a reality in the age to come.

Homesick for Heaven

I began to contemplate people's subconscious longing for a return to Eden when I chanced upon C. S. Lewis' book, *The Weight of Glory*. In this book, Lewis used the word "nostalgia" as a way to describe mankind's natural "desire for our own far-off country," that is, for "Paradise."[5] Nostalgia carries the idea of a wistful or sentimental longing for the past, typically for a time or place with happy, personal memories—but a time or place to which we can never return. I liked the word because it helped me to understand how our human desire for an Edenic paradise is actually linked to its potential fulfillment.

In his book *Wolf Willow*, the late Wallace Stegner described a vivid experience of nostalgia, which was set off by the smell of a native plant called wolf willow. Stegner wrote about his return, as an adult, to a small Canadian town where he lived as a child during the early twentieth century. As he wandered through town reminiscing, he tried to evoke the moods and feelings of his child-hood. Suddenly he caught a scent of wolf willow:

> It is wolf willow, and not the town or anyone in it, that brings me home. For a few minutes, with a handful of leaves to my nose, I look across the clay bank and the hills beyond where the river loops back on itself, enclosing the old sports and picnic ground, and the present and all the years between are shed like a boy's clothes dumped on the bath-house bench. The perspective is what it used to be, the dimensions are restored, the senses are as clear as if they had not been battered with sensation for forty alien years. And the queer adult compulsion to return to one's beginning is assuaged. A contact has been made, a mystery touched. For the moment, reality is made exactly equivalent with memory, and a hunger is satisfied.[6]

Stegner captured the essence of nostalgia when he referred to the "queer adult compulsion to return to one's beginnings." At a deeper level, in terms of the entire human race, the powerful nostalgic urge to reconnect with our past is far more intuitive and deep-rooted than pleasant reminiscences of bygone days. It reveals a subconscious homesickness for something more distant than the span of one's life—or even the span of recorded history. As Lewis suggested, feelings of nostalgia reflect an innate, if shadowy, craving for *Paradise*—a homesickness for the idyllic world that existed long before living memory. It is a yearning for our *intended* home, but one lost to us in the fall—a world to which we long to return but never can.

As Lewis pointed out in his book *Mere Christianity*, however, God has not given the human race any desire that does not have a fulfillment,[7] so our longing for Eden must have the potential to be satisfied. The Bible reveals how. Our desire to return to Eden will be fulfilled in a future, prophesied new heaven and earth, when Jesus returns at the end of this age to establish His eternal Kingdom. Nostalgia, then, as it relates to our longing for a return to Eden, actually looks forward, not backward. It's a conscious longing for a new Paradise where God will once again walk in fellowship with His people (Rev. 21:3). Thus, our collective longing for Eden is in reality a desire for *Heaven*. "'Homesickness for Heaven,'" writes Quaker scholar Arthur Roberts, "pervades stories and rituals of all human cultures, often with no indication of cross-cultural exchanges."[8]

Hints of Eden in Creation

How are feelings of nostalgia evidence for a new heaven and earth? God has graciously given us hints of Eden in creation. Although predators and poisonous snakes and stinging insects dwell in the wilderness, the ecological harmony and beauty of nature still shows a remnant of the peace and tranquility of Eden—and the presence of our Creator.

"We must see nature," Oxford scholar Alister McGrath teaches, "as a continual reminder and symbol of a future renewed creation, a world that we do not yet know but believe to lie over the horizons of our human existence. It is as if we are homesick for a lost Eden, longing for a fulfillment that we know lies ahead of us but have not yet found. . . . We must learn to see the present beauty of nature as a sign and a promise of the coming glory of God, its creator."[9]

The idea of nature as a precursor or foretaste of Heaven (the New Earth) is a concept McGrath reflects on in several of his books. For example, in *A Brief History of Heaven* he writes: "For writers such as Augustine and Lewis, the memory of Eden lingers, haunting humanity with its longing to regain entrance to this forbidden realm. Nature itself becomes a parable, charged with a divinely imbued potential to recreate the memory of Eden, and make us long to return to its now-deserted meadows."[10] Likewise in *The Reenchantment of Nature*: "We journey in hope, knowing that the beauty of this world is a pointer to the glory of the next. . . . Nature is a sign—that it points to something even greater and that at least something of this greater wonder may be known through the natural world."[11] And again in *Glimpsing the Face of God*:

> We appreciate the beauty of a glorious sunset, while wondering if the sense of beauty it awakens within us is somehow a pointer to another and more wonderful world that we have yet to discover . . . ?
>
> What if nature is studded with clues to our true meaning and destiny, and fingerprinted with the presence of God . . . ?
>
> We possess a sense of longing for something that seems to lie beyond the created order, yet is somehow signposted by the creation.[12]

The wonderful, breathtaking good news is that at the end of this age Jesus will return to gather His people to spend eternity with Him in Heaven (1 Thess. 4:16-18). And the Bible reveals that earthly animals will *also* reside there. This brings us to the next chapter. What kinds of animals does the Bible say *will* exist in Heaven? More than you might imagine.

CHAPTER 7

What Kinds of Animals Will Inhabit the New Heaven and Earth?

> *The new creation will stand in a relation of continuity*
> *with the first creation. The creative rule of God will*
> *not destroy the first creation and establish something*
> *entirely different. That would be no fulfillment. . . . The*
> *wilderness [in the New Earth] will remain, to be sure,*
> *for God also loves the alligators and the mountain lions*
> *and wills their fulfillment. But the dream of wilderness*
> *without darkness and violence and pain will come true.*
> H. PAUL SANTMIRE[1]

We saw in chapter five that there will be continuity between Earth today and the future united Heaven with Earth. This *New Earth* will be a world purified of sin and evil, physically transformed, spiritually redeemed, and set free from nature's curse. It will be rich in vegetation, abounding in scenic wonders, and vastly more beautiful than any wilderness or garden our most creative imaginations can conjure up. The New Earth will be, literally, "Heaven on Earth."

What kinds of animals will inhabit this amazing world? We will see in this chapter that it will be populated by the same varieties of animals that dwell on Earth today, but with two major exceptions. First, with the curse removed, there will no longer be predation and death. And second, as a result of this, animals will coexist in perfect tranquilly with redeemed humans and with each other. People and animals will live serenely together with our Lord Jesus Christ in an eternal Peaceable Kingdom—Heaven.

Animals in Heaven

Depending on the interpretation of some Hebrew words, well over one hundred animals are mentioned by name in the Bible.[2] For example, Psalm 104 refers to a stork (and birds in general), wild donkeys, cattle, wild goats, coneys, and lions. Job 39 mentions a doe and fawn, wild ox, ostrich, hawk, and an eagle. Isaiah 60:6 speaks of camels, and numerous passages mention horses. Jesus not only refers to sparrows and ravens, but also several domesticated animals. But will all these varieties of animals inhabit the New Earth (Heaven)?

In light of the evidence we've examined so far, the answer seems almost certainly to be yes. The continuity between our present Earth and the future New Earth provides more than adequate reason to believe that animals dwelling on Earth today will inhabit Heaven. However, there are five more compelling and persuasive biblical evidences I can add to support this conclusion. But first I want to answer a question that will be most dear to many readers: what about pets? Will there be pets in Heaven? Besides the five evidences I'll present below, there is another reason why I strongly believe we'll see our pets in Heaven.

God allows many animals on Earth to be our servants and helpers, as well as our devoted and faithful friends. It would be consistent with God's great love for His people that these animals will continue their role as our friends and companions in the age to come. Our Lord may include pets in Heaven for no other reason than to bless the people who loved and faithfully cared for them in this life. There is nothing in the Bible that should cause us to doubt this. I like the way philosophy professor Peter Kreeft answers this question:

> Would the same animals be in Heaven as on earth? "Is my dead cat in Heaven?" Again, why not? God can raise up the very grass; why not cats? . . . We were meant from the beginning to have stewardship over the animals; we have not fulfilled that divine plan yet on earth; therefore it seems likely that the right relationship with animals will be part of Heaven: proper "pet-ship." And what better place to begin than with already petted pets? [3]

With this note of encouragement, let's consider the five additional evidences that support my claim that pets and other animals will dwell in Heaven alongside redeemed humans.

The Noahic Flood

The first concerns the account of the worldwide Flood. I believe it provides persuasive corroboration that animals presently inhabiting Earth today *will* continue to exist in the restored New Earth.

Prior to the sin-cleansing Flood, God instructed Noah to take into the Ark at least two of every kind of animal that inhabited Earth, at the time (Gen. 7:2-3; 8:19). God didn't recreate animals after the Flood, He preserved those that already existed to repopulate Earth: "Then God said to Noah, 'Come out of the ark, you and your wife and your sons and their wives. Bring out every kind of living creature that is with you—the birds, the animals, and all the creatures that move along the ground—so they can multiply on the earth and be fruitful and increase in number upon it'" (Gen. 8:15-17). Would God have preserved this incredible menagerie of animals from the judgment of the great Flood, and then not allow the same kinds of animals to inhabit the New Earth when He removes the curse and redeems creation in the eschaton? Not doing so would seem incompatible with God's great love for the animals He created, protected on the ark, and used to repopulate Earth.

Here's another way to see this. The apostle Peter contrasts the "destruction" of Earth during to the Noahic Flood with the future judgment of Earth prior to God establishing a "new heaven and earth" (2 Pet. 3:3-13). If the great Flood *prefigures* God's ultimate end-time judgment of Earth, along with the redemption of saved humanity, surely the same kinds of animals that embarked from the ark with Noah and his family will be included in the New Earth—especially since creation's redemption is tied directly to human redemption (Rom. 8:18-25), as we'll see in the following chapter.

The Peaceable Kingdom

Hanging on my study wall is a reproduction of a Native American painting reflecting the Peaceable Kingdom (derived from Isaiah 11:6-9). In the Isaiah passage, children live safely among wolves, lions, bears, poisonous snakes, and other dangerous animals. In my painting, the visual message is the same, but the scene is entirely different. The background is rugged Southwest desert. The animals include a peccary, Gila monster, armadillo, skunk, rattlesnake, jackrabbit, porcupine, mountain lion, and other animals indigenous to the American Southwest. All of the animals are huddled around a Navajo child who is hugging a coyote. The coyote is cuddling a lamb. I love this painting because it reminds me that God's eternal Kingdom—Heaven—will embrace a vast pageantry of created life from around the globe, including the wild creatures living in their native habitats around my Southern California home. Here's the passage Isaiah penned, and my Native American painting replicates:

In that day the wolf and the lamb will live together; the leopard and the goat will be at peace. Calves and yearlings will be safe among lions, and a little child will lead them all. The cattle will graze among bears. Cubs and calves will lie down together. And lions will eat grass as the livestock do. Babies will crawl safely among poisonous snakes. Yes, a little child will put its hand in a nest of deadly snakes and pull it out unharmed. Nothing will hurt or destroy in all my holy mountain. And as the waters fill the sea, so the earth will be filled with people who know the LORD. (Isa. 11:6-9—NLT).

Isaiah wrote this passage around seven centuries before the birth of Christ, and it eloquently reveals one of the most incredible and wonderful features of the future Messianic Kingdom. More than any other passage in Scripture, it provides a tantalizing glimpse of what the relationship between humans and the animal kingdom will be like on the New Earth—as well as the relationship that will exist among animals themselves. This passage is also consistent with the prophet Hosea's prediction that in the last days—in the new heaven and earth—God will make a covenant with the animal kingdom (Hos. 2:18).

The Isaiah and Hosea passages further confirm that earthly animals will one day dwell in Heaven. Since the Peaceable Kingdom is a fundamental feature of the New Earth, it clearly shows that the animals living on Earth today will be the same varieties that populate Heaven.

Jesus Anticipated the Peaceable Kingdom

What is most striking about the Isaiah passage is the incredible transformation that will occur in order for humans and domesticated animals to live peacefully with wild predators and poisonous snakes. Moreover, not only will dangerous animals become harmless to people, but there will also be reconciliation among animals themselves—between wild and domesticated animals and between predators and prey. As Bible scholar Richard Bauckham points out, the Isaiah passage "is a picture of reconciliation of the human world with the wild world, healed of the fear and violence that had been accepted, as a pragmatic compromise, in the Noahic Covenant" (see Gen. 9:2-3).[4]

Bauckham then makes an intriguing observation that's worth considering: "It is likely that the ecotopia envisaged in Isaiah 11 is the key to understanding the reference to wild animals in Mark's brief account of Jesus in the wilderness"[5] This is a third reason for why we can expect earthly animals to dwell in Heaven. Here's the passage Bauckham is referring to:

> At once the Spirit sent him [Jesus] out into the desert, and he was in the desert forty days, being tempted by Satan. He was *with the wild animals,* and angels attended him (Mark 1:12-13; emphasis added).

Linking the Isaiah 11 passage with Mark 1:13, Bauckham continues: "Jesus in the wilderness enacts, in an anticipatory way, the peace between the human world and wild nature that is the Bible's hope for the messianic future. Mark's simple but effective phrase ('he was with the wild animals') has no suggestion of hostility or resistance about it. It indicates Jesus' peaceable presence with the animals. . . ."[6]

Elsewhere Bauckham explains that Jesus being "with the wild animals" carries the idea of having a close association or friendship with them: "Mark 1:13 depicts Jesus enjoying the peaceable harmony with wild animals which had been God's original intention for humanity."[7] In other words, Bauckham believes that Jesus' time with wild animals in the wilderness portends the fulfillment of Old Testament hopes for peace between humans and wild animals in the "messianic future."[8] His evidence for this centers on an understanding of wild animals in Jewish tradition: "The Jewish tradition, against which Mark 1:13 should be read, saw the enmity of wild animals as a distortion of the created relationship of humans and wild animals and the result of human sin."[9] Thus, as the prophesized "Davidic Messiah," Jesus in the wilderness "inaugurates the messianic age not only by overcoming Satan, but also by establishing the [future] messianic peace with wild animals."[10]

If Bauckham's analysis is correct, we have at the beginning of the oldest gospel a glimpse, through the eyes of the Messiah, of the prophesied Peaceable Kingdom; evidence from Jesus Himself that animals will dwell on the New Earth.

Animals Praise God

The fourth biblical evidence that animals will inhabit the New Earth, from Revelation 5:11-14, is the Bible's portrayal of them praising God in Heaven and on Earth alongside angelic beings and humans. Verse 13 states:

> Then I [the apostle John] heard every creature in heaven and on earth and under the earth and on the sea, and all that is in them, singing:
> "To him who sits on the throne and to the
> Lamb [Jesus]
> be praise and honor and glory and power,
> for ever and ever!"

Several books in the Old Testament also portray animals praising God, especially the Psalms. In Psalm 150:6 (the last verse in the last Psalm), the Psalmist cries out for "everything that has breath [to] praise the LORD." In fact other Psalms make it clear that *all* of creation—not just humans, angels and animals—acknowledge and praise the Creator (see Ps. 65:12-13; 69:34; 96:11-12; 103:22; 145:10).

That non-human life is revealed praising God on Earth *and* in Heaven further illustrates the continuity of animal life between our present Earth and the restored New Earth. It seems unlikely animals would be portrayed in Scripture praising God on Earth and in Heaven if God were going to exclude them from the joy and bliss of the future New Earth.

The most comprehensive Psalm portraying animal life praising God is Psalm 148. Here rulers of nations, men, women, children, angels, and *all* of creation, both living and inanimate, are called upon to "Praise the LORD from the heavens" (1) and to "praise the LORD from the earth" (7). This includes "great sea creatures and all ocean depths . . . wild animals and all cattle, small creatures and flying birds" (7, 10). Even trees, rain, wind, mountains, and the sun and moon are told to praise their Creator (3, 4, 8-9).

This probably needs clarification. In the future transformed New Earth, it may be that animals can somehow communicate with humans (we'll explore this possibility in chapter ten). But in this age and on Earth now, passages describing animals and inanimate things voicing praises to God should be considered personifications. Nevertheless, and this is the point, these passages communicate the reality that *all* creatures bring glory and enjoyment to God simply by fulfilling the purpose of their creation—a purpose that will continue on and reach perfection in the Peaceable Kingdom. Professor Bauckham has researched and written extensively on the future relationship between humans and the rest of creation. Here's his thought on this:

When modern Christians encounter the theme of all creation's worship of God in Psalm 148 or in other passages of Scripture, they are apt not to take it very seriously. They may take it to reflect some kind of pre-scientific animism or pan-psychism that attributes rational consciousness to all things, even mountains, rain, and trees. Or they may take it to be mere poetic fancy. Both reactions miss the significance of this biblical theme. These passages about creation's praise are, of course, metaphorical: they attribute to non-human creatures the human practice of praising God in language (or in the case of trees in Isa. 55:12, clapping their hands!). But the metaphor points to a reality: all creatures bring glory to God simply by being themselves and fulfilling their God-given roles in God's creation.[11]

Otherworldly Creatures

The fifth biblical evidence that animals will inhabit the New Earth, and one often overlooked, is the presence of otherworldly animals praising God in Heaven:

> Also before the throne there was what looked like a sea of glass, clear as crystal.
>
> In the center, around the throne were four living creatures, and they were covered with eyes, in front and in back. The first living creature was like a lion, the second was like an ox, the third had a face like a man, the fourth was like a flying eagle. Each of the four living creatures had six wings and was covered with eyes all around, even under his wings. Day and night they never stop saying:
> "Holy, holy, holy
> is the Lord God Almighty,
> who was, and is, and is to come." (Rev. 4:6-8)

In his book *Living with Other Creatures*, professor Bauckham analyzes the four living creatures described in this passage. Although these "heavenly creatures" are obviously "superior to all earthly creatures," they worship God, Bauckham declares, as representatives "on behalf of the whole animate creation, human and non-human."[12] If the four living creatures resemble earthly creatures, continues Bauckham, "such an interpretation would suggest that each living creature represents one major category of the animate creation: the living creature like a lion represents the wild land animals, the one like an ox represents domestic land animals, the one like an eagle represents birds, and the one with a face like a human face represents humans."[13]

Actually, several interpretations have been given concerning these four creatures. Some consider them to symbolize attributes of God. Other commentators see them as angels representing *all* creation. Still others, such as Bauckham, believe they specifically correspond to animate creation. Regardless of their actual identity, these creatures represent, as Bauckham noted when referring to animals praising God in Psalm 148, "The reality . . . that all creatures bring glory to God simply by being themselves and fulfilling their God-given roles in God's creation."[14] This would suggest that even if these creatures are only representative or symbolic, they still point toward the existence in Heaven of the animals they represent.

Randy Alcorn, in his acclaimed book *Heaven*, also comments on the four living creatures, but he considers them to be more than merely symbolic. Rather, they are actual otherworldly *animals*. The passage says the four living creatures are *like* four kinds of earthy animals. The Greek word for "creature" in this passage is *zoon*, which refers to living animals and is where we get the word "zoo." In the King James Version, the "living creatures" are translated "beast." Alcorn writes,

Somehow we have failed to grasp that the "living creatures" who cry out "Holy, holy, holy" are *animals*—living, breathing, intelligent and articulate *animals* who dwell in

God's presence, worshiping and praising him. . . . Perhaps they're the prototype creatures of Heaven after whom God designed Earth's animals. But even though they're highly intelligent and expressive, they're still animals; that's what Scripture calls them. . . .

Although earthly animals aren't capable of verbalizing praise as these animals in Heaven do, the passages speaking of earthly animals praising God . . . clearly suggest that animals have a spiritual dimension far beyond our understanding. The Bible tells us that animals, in their own way, praise God. By extending to them the blessing of mankind's redemption [Rom. 8:19-23], just as he extended to them the curses of mankind's sin, God will grant them an important role on the New Earth.

Once we recognize that the living creatures are animals, we need not see other references to animals in the present Heaven as figurative.[15]

Alcorn makes two important points. First, animals *will live* "on the New Earth." Second, they will reside on the New Earth *because* God extends to animals "the blessings of mankind's redemption." Old Testament professor Daniel Block agrees: "The inclusion of these [four living] creatures with the twenty-four elders before the throne and the Lamb suggest they represent redeemed creation." Commenting on Revelation 5:13, Block adds: "This vision of a redeemed cosmos includes all creatures, with all their territorial and biological diversity, giving eternal praise to the Creator."[16]

Regardless of the actual identity of these creatures, that biblical revelation shows them praising God in Heaven alongside angels and accompanied by "every creature . . . on earth and under the earth and on the sea, and all that is in them " (Rev. 5:11-14) is strong evidence that animals will dwell in the eschatological New Earth. It seems unlikely the Bible would describe animals praising

God in Heaven and on Earth in such detail if they were not going to be included in the everlasting Kingdom.

No Teddy Bears in Heaven

One more thing before moving on, and this is more of a personal note than a biblical comment.

As we saw, Isaiah envisioned a future renewed Earth where creation's curse is removed and humans and animals coexist peacefully together. No doubt, as Isaiah portrays, wolves and lambs will get along, bears and calves will play together, and people will live safely among snakes. But I believe the relationship between humans and animals in the New Earth will be much more exciting. Yes, people and animals will peaceably coexist, but I don't think Isaiah's illustration should be interpreted to mean that human/animal relationship will be one of continuous playtime and hugging. Animals will not become living teddy bears in the New Earth. They will still be animals with their own identities and distinct personalities.

One of my favorite joys when hiking wild country is anticipating unexpected encounters with wild animals living in their native habitats. If all I had to do is walk outdoors and find wildlife eagerly waiting to be petted . . . well, that wouldn't be much fun. *Wild*-life is what makes the wilderness wild, and since the New Earth will be an improvement on even Eden, I believe we will still experience the joy of finding and observing wildlife in wild habits. Certainly we will have opportunities to touch, play, and even pet bears, wolves, and other creatures that were potentially dangerous on this Earth, but I believe (and hope) that animals in the New Earth will maintain an independence similar to what they enjoy on our old Earth. Perhaps the major difference between Earth today and the future New Earth is that no animal will be dangerous or terrify us—nor will we be a danger to or terrify them!

Will There Be *Resurrected* Animals in Heaven?

In light of all the biblical evidence we've examined in this and the previous chapters, I believe I've presented a compelling case that the eschatological New Earth (Heaven) will not only be inhabited by redeemed humans, angelic beings, and, of course, our Lord Jesus Christ, but also by animals. The question now is where exactly do the animals that will dwell in Heaven come from? There seems to be only three possibilities, one of them being that God will *resurrect* animals that have lived and died on this Earth to populate the New Earth. I believe this is exactly what will happen, and I'll present my case in the next two chapters.

Part Three

Animal Resurrection and the Possibility of "Talking" with Animals in Heaven

CHAPTER 8

Will Our Pets and Other Animals Be Resurrected?

When I was in my early teens, Billy Graham had a syndicated column in newspapers across America. I only remember reading one article, but it has stuck in my mind for more than a half century. A child wrote the great evangelist to ask if his puppy would go to Heaven. With compassionate sensitivity, Graham replied (in essence), "If it's necessary for your puppy to be in Heaven in order for you to be happy there, then yes, he'll be in Heaven." Graham gave a perfect answer for the child, but it is somewhat ambiguous for adults wondering the same thing. In this chapter, I'm going to be specific: It's God's *plan* for our pets to be reunited with us in Heaven—as well as wild and domesticated animals.

My family and I have raised—and buried—four dog friends over a span of more than forty years. My kids literally grew up with the first one, my wife's large and lovable Golden Retriever, Bear. He shared our lives for over eleven years—hiking, camping, playing, jogging, and just hanging out. As I shared in the introduction to this book, Bear died on our twentieth wedding anniversary, while my wife and I were out of town. Only my son and daughter were home to comfort Bear as he was dying. At the time my son was fifteen years old, and he had the heartbreaking task of burying his canine "brother," something he'll never forget and something that still brings tears to my eyes when I think about it after all these years.

People who have raised and buried dogs, cats, and other pets know exactly how we felt loosing Bear. Pets become family. And like anyone who dies that is close to us, we find consolation in the hope that someday we'll be reunited with our pets "on the other side." But let's admit it. For most people, the hope that we'll see our pets in Heaven is based more on wishful desire than confident assurance. Quaker scholar Arthur Roberts voiced this sentiment when he spoke about his own uncertainty on the resurrection of animals. He wrote, "This bothers me a bit, for I've had several dogs I'd like to see again, and a horse—Eagle was his name—I'd really love to ride once more across an Idaho pasture on a bright Saturday morning."[1]

This brings us to the very heart of this study: Will pets, like God's people, be *resurrected* and reunited with their human companions in the future New Earth (Heaven)? Likewise, will sentient wild animals roaming Earth today also resurrect and live without fear of humans (and each other) in the same Peaceable Kingdom? I believe the answer to both questions is yes. The purpose of this chapter, then, is to demonstrate beyond reasonable doubt that earth-bound animals will be resurrected.

What We've Learned

Let's begin by summarizing what we've learned so far. In chapter one, we saw that God loves, provides for, values, and derives tremendous joy from the animals He created. This provides a compelling theological basis for assuming that God has more in mind for animals than their short sojourn on Earth. In chapters two through four (part one) and appendix one, we saw that modern studies in animal behavior and brain science support the biblical revelation that animals have souls—and that at least sentient animals have *immortal* souls. In chapters five through seven (part two), we saw that the prophesized New Earth (Heaven) will be inhabited by the same kinds of animals that presently dwell on Earth today.

My goal in part three is to show that these heavenly animals were once earthly animals that lived and died but will one day resurrect to join God's people in Heaven. I'll start by setting the stage theologically and then lay out three credible biblical evidences to support it.

Before the Fall

The Bible tells us that God's created home for Adam and later Eve, as well as their animal companions, was the Garden of Eden (Gen. 2:15-20). As we saw in part two, Eden was a perfect environment, a literal paradise—unspoiled, undefiled, and uncontaminated. Humans and animals lived peacefully together, and both were vegetarians (1:29-30; 2:16). Food was bountiful and readily available (2:19). Most wonderful of all, there was no death in the Garden of Eden and no curse on creation. Thus animals, like humans, had the potential to live forever.

The Fall and Curse of Nature

Sadly, the idyllic garden paradise was lost. This tragic event was set in motion when Adam and Eve rebelled against God and were subsequently banished from Eden. This is referred to as the "Fall," and it impacted all creation. Nature was "cursed" (Gen. 3:17), and evil, suffering, pain, and sin entered the world. From that dreadful day onward, a great gulf began to widen between God's original creation and what it has become today. Hardship and toil became a way of life. Human dominion over animals was no longer peaceful coexistence.[2] After the Fall, the entire human race and all animal life were condemned to live out their lives in a marred, hostile environment; a world plagued by weeds and poisonous plants, diseases and parasites, droughts and famines, raging wildfires and other natural disasters.

God has not told us exactly why nature was cursed and suffers because of human sin, but it makes perfect sense. We know from Scripture that God desires the survival of both humans and animals (Ps. 36:6). We are also told that only people are created in God's image, and that He had the human race in mind when He created Earth (Ps.115:16). Genesis 2:15 adds that God placed Adam and Eve in a perfect natural environment specifically prepared for them, and put nature under their care and management. It would be incongruous for nature to be unaffected when Adam and Eve rebelled against God, opened the door for death and decay to enter the world, and were expelled from the Garden as part of their punishment.

What's important to see here is that nature itself is not sinful; it did not fall. Nature was *cursed* due to Adam and Eve's rebellion against God (Gen. 3:17; cf. Rom. 8:19-21), and to this day it's the victim of bad human choices. As theologian Hanlee Barnette put it, "Man's sin against God pulled nature down along with man."[3] The great Reformation theologian John Calvin agrees. In his commentary on Romans 8:20-22, he writes, "all created things, both on earth and in the invisible heavens, which are in themselves blameless, undergo punishment for our sins; for it has come about that they are liable to corruption not through their own fault. Thus the condemnation of mankind is imprinted on the heaven, and on the earth, and on all creatures."[4]

Down through the ages, numerous other Christian theologians have commented on how the Fall affected animal life. Fifteenth century reformer, Martin Luther, pointed out that along with "thorns, thistles, vermin, flies, [and] toads . . . the savagery of wild animals were part of the punishment for human sin."[5] Eighteenth century English theologian John Wesley taught that animals were innocent victims of the Fall. Their vulnerability to predation, disease, parasites, plagues, starvation, crippling accidents, and other calamities were directly linked to the rebellion and iniquity of Adam and Eve. Creatures "could not sin," wrote Wesley, "for they were not moral agents. Yet how severe do they suffer!—yea, many of them, beasts of burden in particular, almost the whole time of their abode on Earth."[6]

Because nature's curse and the consequent plight of its wild inhabitants is tied directly to human sin, its release from the curse is wholly dependent upon mankind's redemption. This brings us to the first biblical evidence confirming animal resurrection.

Nature's Redemption

Chapter six describes the physical environment of the future New Earth as similar to the Garden of Eden—only more wonderful. What ushers in this renewed creation? The Bible tells us that it will come about with the future redemption of God's people. Our redemption initiates nature's redemption; it provides the basis upon which the curse is removed and nature is restored to its pre-Fall state. The Apostle Paul speaks to this in Romans chapter eight:

> Yet what we suffer now is nothing compared to the glory he [God] will give us later. For all creation is waiting eagerly for that future day when God will reveal who his children really are. Against its will, everything on earth was subjected to God's curse. All creation anticipates the day when it will join God's children in glorious freedom from death and decay. For we know that all creation has been groaning as in the pains of childbirth right up to the present time. And even we Christians, although we have the Holy Spirit within

us as a foretaste of future glory, also groan to be released from pain and suffering. We, too, wait anxiously for that day when God will give us our full rights as his children, including the new bodies he has promised us (8:18–23 NLT).

Biblical theology and church tradition agree that human redemption will include the whole of creation. This is the great message expressed by Paul in the passage above, as well as a theme in Old Testament prophecies. Moreover, this belief is expressed in the theologies of many early church Fathers, such as Justin, Irenaeus, Lactantius, and others,[7] as well as by recent theologians and scholars (as we'll see in the next chapter). The question is, how exactly will creation's redemption—the removal of the curse and restoration to Eden-like conditions—be linked to *human* redemption, as the apostle Paul expresses above? In particular, for the purpose of this book, how will human redemption play out in the resurrection of animals?

The answer is simple but incredibly wonderful. As with humans, creation's redemption depends on the work of Christ. Now, I'm *not* saying Jesus died for animals the same as He died for humans. When Jesus died for the sins of the world (John 1:29; Rom. 5:8), it paved the way for the salvation of *people* who receive Him as Lord and Savior (John 1:12). But I *am* saying that the Bible teaches, as Paul explains in Romans eight, that the damage wrought on creation by fallen humanity (the curse) will be removed with the redemption of God's people. All creation, Paul declares, "is waiting eagerly" for its redemption alongside saved humanity, when it will finally "join God's children in glorious freedom from death and decay" (Rom. 8:19-21).

Other passages confirm this. Paul writes in Ephesians that God "made known to us the mystery of his will according to his good pleasure, which he purposed in Christ, to be put into effect when the times will have reached their fulfillment—to bring *all things in heaven and on earth* together under one head, even Christ" (1:9-10, emphasis added). Similarly, Colossians chapter one tells us that God reconciled "to himself *all things*, whether things on *earth* or things in heaven, by making peace through his [Jesus'] blood, shed on the cross" (1:20, emphasis added). In Revelation God said, "I am making *everything* new" (21:5) and "no longer will there be any curse" (22:3). *All* things mean *all* things and *everything* includes *everything*. Not just Christ's followers, but the entire Earth and cosmos cursed by human sin will be made new. Every animal and plant and every natural feature despoiled and polluted by the human race will be restored. Ecological theologian H. Paul Santmire said it this way: "Christ is the royal minister God sends to redeem creation . . . [and] the royal minister God sends to inaugurate the new creation."[8]

It makes perfect theological sense that God will redeem creation through human redemption. Remember, animals did not sin and nature did not fall when Adam and Eve disobeyed God and were banished from the Garden of Eden. Nature was *cursed* because of the first couple's sinful rebellion—and to this day it continues to suffer because of human sin. In the case of people, those who accept salvation offered by Jesus Christ are granted forgiveness of sins (redemption) and promised eternal resurrected bodies in Heaven.

But what about animals? Will they be resurrected as part of creation's redemption? The biblical evidence indicates they will. Because nature's curse is tied directly to human sin and is removed by human redemption, it follows naturally that animals sharing that redemption will likewise be resurrected along with God's people. Why would God give humans such glorious grace and not the animals whose curse people are responsible for? If all creation is redeemed alongside saved humanity, it logically and theologically follows that animals will also be resurrected!

In other words, since creation anticipates freedom from bondage to the curse through the redemption of God's people—and

God's people receive resurrected bodies, as Paul taught in Romans 8, 1 Corinthians 15, and elsewhere—we have good theological reason to believe that animals participating in that redemption will likewise receive imperishable, resurrected bodies along with redeemed humanity. Thus, animals that have lived and died on Earth will be resurrected to dwell in the New Earth—Heaven. This brings us to the second evidence confirming animal resurrection.

The Best Option Is Resurrection

We saw in chapter seven that animals will definitely dwell in the restored New Earth. So skeptics who reject animal resurrection must still account for the origin of these animals. Could these creatures have an origin other than resurrection? Or is the resurrection of earthly animals the best explanation for the source of the animals that will inhabit the New Earth? Besides resurrection, there are only two other options. Eliminating them confirms that the origin of *heavenly* animals must be resurrected *earthly* animals.

The first option is that the animals inhabiting the New Earth are the same kinds of animals dwelling on Earth today, but *recreated* anew for Heaven. In other words, the same *varieties* of animals, but not the same ones actually living today and later resurrected to dwell in Heaven. It could be argued, however, that this view seems inconsistent with God's righteous judgment. Rather than recreating the same kinds of animals now living on Earth and placing them in Heaven, it seems more likely that God will resurrect existing animals, which for no fault of their own are innocent victims of mankind's sin (i.e. the curse—Gen. 3). Furthermore, nowhere does the Bible suggest that God will recreate the same kinds of animals now living on Earth to populate the restored New Earth. He didn't do this after the sin-cleansing Flood during Noah's time—He preserved *existing* animals to repopulate Earth. Why would God do any differently in the restored New Earth?

A second possibility is that the animals that will inhabit the New Earth are *different kinds* of animals than today's earthly varieties. God could create entirely new species of animals specifically designed for Heaven. The problem with this theory is that there is no biblical precedent for making such a claim; nowhere in Scripture is there a hint that God will create new varieties of animals in the eschaton. The animals the Bible mentions that will dwell in the "new heaven and earth" are the same kinds of animals presently inhabiting Earth today (e.g. Isa.11:6-8). When Jesus makes His grand appearance prior to the final events in Revelation, He will be riding on a white *horse* (19:11)—not on a unicorn!

The third option is the most likely. The animals that will reside in Heaven are those that have died under the curse, redeemed with the rest of creation, and resurrected with saved humanity at the end of this age. This is even more probable in light of the biblical revelation that God has given at least sentient animals *immortal* souls, as was demonstrated in chapter four.

Look at it like this. Why would God give animals' immortal souls if they are *not* going to be resurrected in imperishable, physical bodies? I believe He gave animals immortal souls precisely because they *will* be resurrected! If the redemption of God's people includes resurrected bodies in the age to come, it reasonably follows that soul-bearing animals—which will share in the same redemption—will also be given resurrected bodies. This is not only consistent with God's great love for and enjoyment of the animals He created to inhabit Earth, but it's also consistent with divine justice—a third evidence for animal resurrection.

Divine Justice

This evidence has to do with divine recompense for the suffering animals endured in this life. Theologian John Wesley expressed hope in a "general deliverance" of animals where they will be compensated after death for the suffering they endured on Earth. In other words, as Randy Alcorn explains, since animals experience pain and suffering due to human sin, it "seems to require that some animals who lived, suffered, and died on the old Earth must be made whole on the New Earth."[9] Other theologians agree. "Many Christian thinkers," writes philosopher Michael Murray, "have argued that animal immortality plays an important role in explaining the reality of animal pain and suffering in the earthy life. Perhaps there is a connection between the earthly life of animals, filled as it is with pain and suffering, and a blissful, eternal existence ['as resurrected beings'] for those animals in the divine presence."[10] In short, God will grant animals eternal existence in resurrected bodies to compensate for the suffering they endured in this life, for no fault of their own, due to creation's curse brought on by sinful humanity.

The argument that God's love and justice will embrace animal resurrection is a legitimate biblical position. Christian theologian Andrew Linzey, who has written books and articles on animals and Christianity, sums it like this: "The issue of suffering and evil endured by animals makes the question central to theodicy [justifying divine goodness in light of evil]. However we may construe the origins of evil in the world, a just and loving God must in the last analysis be able to offer recompense and redemption commensurate with the evil that has been endured."[11] I see no better way for this to happen than resurrection into eternal life in the Peaceable Kingdom.

What about Mosquitos, Goldfish, Toads, and Snakes?

After sharing in a Bible study my belief that pets and other animals will inhabit Heaven, someone asked me if mosquitos will also be there? It was a good question, and not the first time I've been asked if simple creatures will be in Heaven? Where *does* God draw the line? Will just pets be in Heaven? Will only mammals be resurrected? What about birds and reptiles? And the most unlikely candidates of all, what about the trillions of insects, spiders, and bugs that have already lived and died on Earth? Will they be in Heaven? Even Christians who firmly believe pets will be resurrected have a hard time getting their minds around the image of insects and spiders lurking in Heaven.

Simple creatures overwhelmingly comprise the vast majority of animals that live or have lived on Earth. So the question of whether or not they will be in the New Earth, and especially resurrected, deserves an honest answer.

C. S. Lewis would respond to this question by pointing out that lower forms of animals will *not* be resurrected because "immortality has almost no meaning for a creature which is not 'conscious,'" and only higher animals possess "selfhood."[12] In other words, since only sentient animals (those that are able to learn, perceive, and feel things) possess selfhood, biologically less complex varieties of animals will not be resurrected. I have three responses to this.

First, as we saw in chapter three, during the past few decades a tremendous amount of new data on animals' mental abilities has been discovered. These studies reveal that animal emotions and cognition are far more sophisticated than previously assumed. Were he alive today, C. S. Lewis (who died in 1963) may well broaden his category of what kinds of animals are "conscious" and therefore (by his standard) will be resurrected. Today, it's well-known that many animals once thought to be little more than biological machines, which functioned merely on instinct, possess surprisingly well-developed mental abilities.

My second response is to challenge the *assumption* that only complex animals will inhabit the New Earth because it's based entirely on human conjecture. It assumes that the eternal destiny of nonhuman life is in accord with *our* personal feelings and opinions—not on what may or may not be God's decision. Who knows if God will allow simple organism to inhabit the New Earth except God? Let me put this more precisely.

Although the evidence we've examined throughout this book justly concludes that at least sentient animals will enjoy Heaven in resurrected bodies, only God knows if the lower classifications of animals will dwell there. Skeptics need to understand that the fate of insects, spiders, fish, amphibians, and other barely sentient creatures is not determined by people's opinions but by God. He can certainly grant even the simplest animals eternal life in the age to come, if He chooses to do so. No one can justify denying this. (Of course, regardless of whether or not less complex animals are in Heaven, it has nothing to do with the fact that sentient animals *will be* resurrected.)

Having said this, I believe there is good reason to believe that even simple creatures may dwell in Heaven. The only "qualification" for animal resurrection seems to be (since they are not fallen) that God gives them eternal souls that can survive physical death. The Bible doesn't restrict what kinds of animals possess souls; it only teaches that animals have souls (see chapter four). "All living animals have souls if they have organic life," explains theologian and scholar J. P. Moreland, "regardless of the degree to which they are conscious."[13] So according to Moreland, even animals without a conscious life have souls.

Since possessing a soul is essential for resurrection, and all animals possess souls, I see no biblical reason why *all* earthly animals, including non-sentient creatures, wouldn't inhabit Heaven. The prophet Hosea speaks of a future covenant that God will make with restored Israel in the Messianic Age (the new heaven and new earth; Isa. 65:17-25). It will include "beasts of the field" and "birds of the sky" and "the creeping things of the ground" (Hos. 2:18; NASB). Animals creeping on the ground are mostly reptiles, amphibians, insects, and bugs!

My third response to the assumption that less complex creatures will not dwell on the New Earth is this: God may grant non-sentient animals eternal life for His own good pleasure—and for the pleasure they will bring His people. It's hard to imagine a redeemed and restored New Earth without butterflies and ladybugs gracing flowers; frogs croaking from ponds while damselflies hover above them; lizards basking placidly on sun-soaked rocks; and the countless other simple creatures that add beauty to nature and delight humans of all ages. And of course the animals we consider dangerous or vermin on Earth today—if dwelling on the New Earth—will no longer be harmful or distasteful to us.

If the New Earth is more glorious and beautiful than our present Earth, surely the creatures that contribute so much to the beauty, wonder, ecological harmony, and magnificence of wild nature will inhabit Heaven. Perhaps the ultimate answer to the question of whether or not simple varieties of animals will inhabit Heaven is—why wouldn't they? I know of no biblical reason or persuasive argument why they won't.

CHAPTER 9

Bible Scholars Who Believe in the Probability of Animal Resurrection

Not long ago a *USA Today* article reported that Pope Francis allegedly believes dogs can go to Heaven: "During a recent public appearance, Francis comforted a boy whose dog had died, noting, 'One day, we will see our animals again in the eternity of Christ. Paradise is open to all of God's creatures.'"[1] Although the magazine later recanted the factual nature of the story, calling it an "urban legend" and crediting the quote to a version of a quotation uttered by Pope Paul VI (who died in 1978),[2] we can be certain it generated a lot of excitement among pet owners and animal rights advocates. In particular, it revealed the desire of many animal lovers to have support from well-known Christian leaders that they will see their beloved pets in the afterlife.

Despite the apocryphal nature of the quote, it points to another persuasive reason why I believe animals will be resurrected: There are *legitimate* writings from Christian scholars, in particular Reformation and post-Reformation theologians, who *do* believe in animal resurrection. When great Christian thinkers—men and women who spend much of their lives studying and teaching theological issues—agree that animals will probably be resurrected, it's persuasive corroboration that they will. The fact is belief in the probability of animal resurrection is not without endorsement from well-respected theologians and scholars. The following are examples of some of the most well-known.

Martin Luther. The great Reformation theologian Martin Luther considered the value of animals primarily by how they benefited people. Nevertheless, like many other Christian theologians, he viewed animals as "hapless, innocent victims" of the Fall.[3] Does this mean Luther believed animals would be recompensed for their suffering in this life and resurrected to inhabit the restored New Earth? I'm not aware if Luther made this theological connection, but on a personal level he seemed to endorse animal resurrection. Here's what Luther had to say on the subject.

When asked if he believed dogs, in particular his dog Tólpel, would be in Heaven, he is reported to have answered, "Certainly, for there the earth will not be without form and void. Peter said that the last day would be the restitution of all things. God will create a new heaven and a new earth and new Tólpel with hide of gold and silver. God will be all in all; and snakes, now poisonous because of original sin, will then be so harmless that we shall be able to play with them."[4] Elsewhere, commenting on Psalm 36:6 ("O Lord, you preserve both man and beast."), Luther remarked that the passage affirms, "that God is rightly called the 'Saviour of all beasts.'"[5]

Martin Luther's apparent optimism that his own pet would survive physical death, his understanding that animals are innocent victims of the Fall, and his acknowledgement that God is "Saviour of all beasts" leads me to believe that Luther probably believed that animals alive today will live on in the New Earth. Professor Murray agrees: "Martin Luther appears to have held that at least some animals are immortal."[6]

John Calvin. Another Reformation scholar and theologian who acknowledged the probability of animal resurrection is John

Calvin. He observed "that nonhuman animals long to partici-
pate in . . . redemption,"[7] and made a provocative statement in
"Speculation About Animals" that implies he believed in animal
resurrection: "Because the creatures . . . have a hope of being freed
hereafter from corruption, it follows that they groan like a woman
in labour until they have been delivered. . . . In short, the creatures are not content with their present condition, and yet they do
not pine away irremediably. They are, however, in labour, *because
they are waiting to be renewed to a better state*" (emphasis added).[8] In
his Commentary on Romans, Calvin wrote, "I understand the passage [8:19] to have this meaning—that there is no element and no
part of the world which is being touched, as it were, with a sense
of its present misery, that does not intensely hope for resurrection."[9] Concerning verse 20 he continues: "No part of the universe
is untouched by the longing with which everything on this world
aspires to the hope of resurrection."[10]

John Wesley. Probably no well-known theologian has expressed
a greater and more passionate belief that animals will resurrect
than the eighteenth century Anglican clergyman, evangelist, and
cofounder of Methodism, John Wesley. He argued that Romans
8:19-22 implies that the future New Earth would include the exact
same animals that dwell on Earth today. Wesley believed this was
the only way earthly animals could be delivered from the curse.[11]
He "hoped for a 'general deliverance' in which, after death, animals will be compensated for the suffering they underwent and
liberated from the rages of which they partook" on Earth due to
human fallenness.[12] Speaking on animal recompense for their suffering on Earth, Wesley wrote,

> [W]hen God has "renewed the face of the earth," and their
> [animals'] corruptible body has put on incorruption, they
> shall enjoy happiness suited to their state, without alloy,

without interruption, and without end. . . . They [animals] could not sin, for they were not moral agents. Yet how severely do they suffer!—yea, many of them, beasts of burden in particular, almost the whole time of their abode on earth; So [sic] that they can have no retribution here below. But the objection vanishes, if we consider that something better remains after death for these poor creatures also; that these, likewise, shall one day be delivered from this bondage of corruption, and shall then receive an ample amends for all their present sufferings. . . .[13]

Joseph Butler. A contemporary of John Wesley, Anglican bishop and moral philosopher Joseph Butler, who is probably best known for his apologetic refutation of Deism in *The Analogy of Religion*, argues that the evidence for an Intelligent Being (i.e. God) is reflected in the design and creation in nature. He further believed that evidence for Jesus' miraculous resurrection can be drawn from analogies with nature, such as caterpillars "dying" and "resurrected" as butterflies. In the case of animals, Butler "went beyond symbols and analogies . . . and did not hesitate to tout their resurrection in the future as an effect of Christ's resurrection" on a "restored and transformed earth."[14] Butler argued, "Neither can we find anything in the whole analogy of Nature to afford even the slightest presumption that animals ever lose their living powers, much less that they lose them by death."[15]

Peter Kreeft. Answering the question "are there animals in heaven?" well-known contemporary theologian Peter Kreeft makes no bones about his belief in the resurrection of animals:

The simplest answer is: Why not? How irrational is the prejudice that would allow plants (green fields and flowers) but not animals into Heaven . . . .

Would the same animals be in Heaven as on earth? "Is my dead cat in heaven?" Again, why not? God can rise up the very grass; why not cats? . . . We were meant from the beginning to have stewardship over the animals; we have not fulfilled that divine plan yet on earth; therefore it seems likely that the right relationship with animals will be part of Heaven: proper "petship." And what better place to begin than with already petted pets?[16]

Hank Hanegraaff. The president of the Christian Research Institute (AKA "The Bible Answer Man") supports the possibility of animal resurrection:

Scripture does not conclusively tell us whether our pets will make it to heaven. However, the Bible does provide us with some significant clues regarding whether animals will inhabit the new heaven and the new earth. . . .

Furthermore, the Scriptures from first to last suggest that animals have souls. . . . It wasn't until the advent of the seventeenth-century Enlightenment and the thought of Descartes and Hobbes that the existence of animal souls was even questioned in Western civilization. . . .

Finally, while we cannot say for certain that the pets we enjoy today will be "resurrected" in eternity, I, like Joni [EarecksonTada] are not willing to preclude the possibility. Some of the keenest thinkers from C. S. Lewis to Peter Kreeft are not only convinced that animals in general but that pets in particular will be restored in the resurrection. . . .

In the final analysis, one thing is certain: Scripture provides us with a sufficient precedent for suggesting that animals will continue to exist after the return of our Lord.[17]

Randy Alcorn. This popular writer, conference speaker, and author of the highly acclaimed book *Heaven* clearly expects animals to be resurrected:

> We know animals will be on the New Earth, which is a redeemed and renewed old Earth, in which animals had a prominent role. People will be resurrected to inhabit this world. As we saw, Romans 8:21-23 assumes animals as part of a suffering creation eagerly awaiting deliverance through humanity's resurrection. This seems to require that some animals who lived, suffered, and died on the old Earth must be made whole on the New Earth. Wouldn't some of those likely be our pets?[18]

Richard Bauckham. A few years ago I wrote a review of two books written by this British scholar and theologian for the *Christian Research Journal: The Bible and Ecology* and *Living With Other Creatures*.[19] Although Bauckham did not outright state in either book that animals would be resurrected, he did make tantalizing statements that implied they would. For example, he wrote, "If the new creation is the transformation of the whole of this material creation so that all creatures may share in the life of the divine eternity, then Jesus' resurrection must lead the way to new creation for the whole community of creation, not just humans."[20]

In order to get clarification, I emailed Professor Bauckham and asked this question: "What's your belief (and why) on whether or not pets and other animals alive today will be in the new heaven and earth?" Bauckham replied, "I take seriously that the new creation is the new creation of all things. So plants too and rivers and mountains! God will take everything of value into the new creation. Redeemed from all evil and suffering."[21]

C.S. Lewis. This brilliant and gifted scholar is arguably the most widely read and admired Christian apologists in the twentieth century. Apparently, Lewis shared the same concern for the eternal destiny of pets as do many other people. But in his case, he provided a somewhat different—but no less thought-provoking—answer to the issue. In his typical lucid style, Lewis suggested that pets, and perhaps "higher" animals, will experience resurrection and eternal life.

Lewis begins by correctly pointing out that any conclusion about the eternal fate of animals is necessarily speculative because God didn't (or wouldn't) give us that information: "If animals were, in fact, immortal, it is unlikely, from what we discern of God's methods in the revelation, that he would have revealed this truth."[22]

Lewis limited his discussion on animal resurrection to the higher animals, in particular what he refers to as "tame" animals (e.g. pets). He wrote, "The real difficulty about supposing most animals to be immortal is that immortality has almost no meaning for a creature which is not 'conscious'" and functions merely on "a succession of sensations."[23] In the case of higher animals, however, Lewis recognized that they possess "real, though doubtless rudimentary, self-hood . . . and specifically in those we tame . . . [thus] their destiny demands a somewhat deeper consideration."[24]

Lewis' explanation for animal resurrection lies in their interconnectedness with people: "The beasts are to be understood only in their relation to man and, through man, to God." Mankind, Lewis continues, "was appointed by God to have dominion over the beasts, and everything a man does to an animal is either a lawful exercise, or a sacrilegious abuse, of an authority by divine right."[25] Thus, "in so far as the tame animal has a real self or personality, it owes this almost entirety to its master. If a good sheepdog seems 'almost human' that is because a good shepherd has made it so."[26]

Here's how this plays out in terms of animal resurrection. Lewis argued that just as people are "in" Christ, so tame animals "attain a real self . . . *in* their masters. . . . And in this way it seems to me possible that certain animals may have an immortality, not in themselves, but in the immortality of their masters." Moreover, "If any [wild animals] . . . should live again, their immortality would also be related to man—not . . . to individual masters, but to humanity."[27]

In short, Lewis believed human resurrection would encompass "tame" animals because their eternal destiny is directly connected to the people who loved and cared for them. Although Lewis kept his focus primarily on the resurrection of domesticated animals, he allowed that wild animals might also resurrect to inhabit the redeemed New Earth. This is certainly in line with Scripture, which mentions both domesticated and wild animals in the prophesied Peaceable Kingdom (Isa.11:6-9; 65:25).

The Challenge

The Bible clearly reveals that animals have souls (see chapter four). Furthermore, nowhere in the Bible does it say or even imply that animals will not be resurrected. In light of this, I want to end this chapter with six challenges for skeptics to ponder who reject animal resurrection:

- First, if both God and humans enjoy wonderful, heart-felt relationships with animals in this life, why would God remove such blessings in Heaven?
- Second, if this Earth will be redeemed and restored to become the New Earth (Heaven), why would animals not be part of this continuity?
- Third, if Jesus removes the fear and "sting" of death (1 Cor. 15:54-57) and reconciles "all things, whether things

on earth or in heaven" through His atoning work on the cross (Col. 1:20), why would animals not be part of these "all things?"

- Fourth, Paul teaches in Romans chapter eight that all "creation waits in eager expectation" for its redemption (19-21). As part of creation, why would animals be waiting eagerly for their redemption if they are going to be annihilated when Christ returns?

- Fifth, since God created animals with souls, it means they have the potential, like humans, to survive physical death. Why would God endow non-human life with souls if He were not intending to resurrect them in the eschaton?

- Sixth, the Bible reveals that the same kinds of animals inhabiting Earth today will dwell on the New Earth. What better explanation for their origin is there than the resurrection of deceased earth-bound, soul-bearing animals into eternal life in Heaven?

I have yet to hear a persuasive biblical, philosophical, or scientific argument for why animals will not be resurrected to join God's people in Heaven. The pets we love and enjoy in this life, and which serve us faithfully, *will* spend eternity with us. Domesticated animals, whose suffering we are responsible for, *will* be recompensed in the New Earth. The untamed animals that make the wilderness wild *will* roam the forests and fields of the New Earth.

CHAPTER 10

Will People and Animals "Talk" to Each Other in Heaven?

There are more things in heaven and earth, Horatio,
than are dreamt of in your philosophy.
HAMLET, ACT 1, SCENE 5

L et's listen in on a conversation between two characters in Angela Hunt's novel, *Unspoken*:

"You see," she [Nana] kept her eyes trained on Fielding, "in the beginning God created a perfect world, one without death or decay. Oh, he knew what would happen to his creation, never doubt that, but he also knew he would one day redeem the earth and restore the innocence that would be lost . . ."

"I can't prove this"—Nana lowered her gaze as she traced an outline on the lace tablecloth—"but I suspect animals could talk in the days of earth's perfection. Eve didn't seem at all surprised when the serpent spoke to her in the garden. The Bible is filled with verses about how everything in creation praises the Creator—this could be unspoken praise, of course, or perhaps it's a language beyond the range of human hearing. The Bible also tells us of a donkey who spoke—in words—to his master." . . .

"The donkey's speech was a miracle," she said, shrugging, "but maybe the donkey wasn't surprised when he was able to talk." . . .

"Adam learned [to talk] from God," Nana said, her voice firm. "He named all the animals. And someday, when animals repopulate heaven and the new earth, they'll speak again. . . . One day we'll discover that we've been wrong about a lot of things." [1]

Hunt's apparent belief that animals were able to communicate with Adam and Eve in the Garden of Eden—and will do so again in the New Earth (Heaven)—is, of course, speculation. Nor, some will argue, do her two examples of animals speaking adequately support her belief. The serpent that spoke to Eve was the devil masquerading as a serpent, or a symbol of the devil. Either way it was the devil talking to Eve, not a reptile. In the case of the donkey talking to Balaam (see Num. 22: 22-30), it was a miracle, as Nana pointed out—a unique event under special circumstances.

Nevertheless, both examples illustrate that God can allow earthly animals to communicate verbally with humans, if He chooses to do so. In the passage where the donkey spoke to Balaam, God didn't speak through the donkey; the donkey actually spoke *herself* (v. 28). And as Randy Alcorn points out, although the serpent talking to Eve and Balaam's talking donkey "may be figurative language," the "stories are recorded in historical narrative, not in apocalyptic language. Nothing in the context of the Genesis account or the Balaam story indicates these shouldn't be taken literally."[2]

Although unprovable, I believe a case can be made that animals in the New Earth *will* be able to communicate with humans—and a case within acceptable biblical boundaries. It might not be a distinct human-like language, but there may be some kind of communication between resurrected humans and resurrected animals that permits mutual understanding. As I've done throughout this entire book, I'll analyze the evidence for this possibility systematically, step-by-step.

Animals Do Not Instinctively Fear Humans

One of the most delightful insights I've learned in more than forty years of wildlife watching and photography is that many wild animals—although often wary and sometimes skittish around people—are seldom actually terrified of humans, unless they feel threatened.[3] I'm personally convinced that many animals possess an intuition, a "sixth sense," that allows them to be aware of human intentions that go beyond what can be understood through normal sense perception. Hunters, in spite of their expertise in stalking wildlife, frequently return home empty handed while wildlife photographers often "shoot" many outstanding "trophies." A hunter's intention is killing, and I believe many animals somehow realize this.

It's been my experience that when animals sense they are safe around people, many will not immediately dash for cover when we encounter them in the wilds. Research confirms this. There is "good scientific evidence that fear of predators is not hard-wired into animals' brains, but is maintained by ongoing exposure to the risk imposed by predators" (which in the animal world would include humans). In fact the research showed that "fear dissipates in the absence of predators, but that it also returns in areas where predators have been reintroduced."[4]

Similarly, animals accustomed to fearing humans, such as so-called "game animals" hunted by sportsmen (I doubt they're really *game* at all!) generally feel safe and secure in national parks and other areas where hunting is prohibited. Numerous times in Yellowstone National Park I've photographed bison, elk, moose, and other animals from less than a hundred feet away, and they seldom showed any anxiety in my presence. Recently, on a mountain bike ride through an agriculture preserve where no hunting is allowed, I was within a hundred feet of a pack of five coyotes. Rather than dash for cover as coyotes usually do in more hostile environments, they stood for a spell and stared at me before unhurriedly sauntering away. On another mountain biking occasion, this time in a protected state park, a friendly coyote even ran toward me as if he were going to tag along, like one would expect from a neighborhood dog!

Does this lack of intrinsic fear of people point back to a time when humans and animals co-existed peacefully in the Garden of Eden? We know from Scripture that God "brought" animals to Adam to name and to be his companions prior to creating Eve (Gen. 2:18-20). Moreover, there was no predation or eating meat in Eden because humans and animals were vegetarians (1:29-30). The Bible also reveals that animals didn't begin to "fear and dread" humans until after the Noahic Flood, when God gave Noah (and subsequent generations) permission to consume animals (9:2-3). Perhaps animals, like humans, retain a latent, subconscious memory of the peace and companionship that existed in Eden between the first couple and the animal kingdom (see chapter six). This may account for the willingness of many animals to accept our presence—unless they sense we have bad intentions.

All this is to say that the relationship between humans and the animal kingdom was originally designed by God to be one of peaceful coexistence and mutual companionship. If humans and animals shared such a unique relationship in Eden, it shouldn't be surprising that animals may have been able to communicate with the first couple in ways not seen today. This communication may not have been a structured, conventional language corresponding to human language, but a "language" nonetheless, and one both understood. If humans and animals conversed in some fashion in Eden, isn't it reasonable to assume that this ability to communicate will resume in the New Earth—when the enmity and animosity between humans and animals will no longer exist? Perhaps it will.

Animal Archetypes

A familiar ingredient in some myths and religions is that animals can talk. It can be argued from this that in the distant past, beyond conscious memory, humans and animals were somehow able to converse, and a dim memory of this has become ingrained in the mythology and folklores of many cultures. Just as Mesopotamians, Egyptians, Greeks, and other ancient cultures retained in their mythology a latent memory of the Noahic flood, so too myths of humans and animals conversing may actually reflect the historic reality that humans and animals *did* converse in Eden. This phenomenon seems to have been passed on to modern Western culture.

Most of us are familiar with fables and fairy tales that include talking animals, such as *Aesop's Fables* and *Grimm's Fairy Tales*. Likewise, more recent fantasies, such as the characters in Beatrix Potter's books, C. S. Lewis' *The Chronicles of Narnia,* and Edger Rice Burroughs' *Tarzan of the Apes,* include humans and animals talking to each other. And of course people my age remember Donald Duck and his Uncle Scrooge, Mickey Mouse and his girl-friend Minnie, Porky Pig, Bugs Bunny, Woody Woodpecker, and all the other delightful animal characters of the past generations. Similarly, contemporary animated movies and television cartoons carry on the tradition of talking animals.

The belief that some animals can talk is also a characteristic of animism—the religious worldview in all preliterary cultures. A common ingredient in many animistic religions, such as Native Americans before the arrival of Europeans, is the belief that many wild animals not only possess emotions and have the ability to reason, but can speak (although normally they remain silent).

Could the presence of talking animals in fables, fairy tales, fantasies, cartoons, and some religions actually be *archetypes* of creatures that really did exist and were capable of communicating with humans? Perhaps they are.

Remnants of the Ability to Communicate with Animals Remain

If humans and animals were able to communicate in the Garden of Eden, the trait was lost after Adam and Eve's banishment from Eden. The first couple's sin and rebellion against God resulted in their estrangement from God, nature's curse, and the subsequent enmity that arose between humans and the natural world (Gen. 3). This understandably would have squelched most, if not all, human/animal communication. Nevertheless, it appears that remnants of the ability of humans and animals to communicate with each other seem to remain—especially on the animal side of the equation. Here's an example that many readers will recognize.

Anyone who has studied animal behavior—or has raised a dog or cat—knows that most animals possess one or more senses that are far superior to humans'. Many animals can see things, hear noises, and smell scents far beyond the capabilities of human sense organs. Some also seem to possess the "sixth sense" I mentioned earlier, which is the ability to understand people's intentions in a way not directly related to their five senses.

While modern societies have isolated people from nature, degrading any latent ability we may have possessed to understand the thoughts and intentions of wild creatures in Eden, many animals have not totally lost that ability with regard to humans. Observant pet owners frequently noticed an intuition and alertness in their animal companions, which surfaces under some circumstances. Dogs will often display caution and suspicion around certain strangers—which we later learn are unscrupulous or even dangerous—while being accepting and friendly with other strangers. As researcher Jeffery Kluger put it in *The Animal Mind*, "Dogs . . . read humans well. There's a lot of research on that."[5]

It appears that a few people also possess a similar intuition into the minds of animals. Terri Irwin, wife of the late Steve Irwin, who had a television program on Animal Planet, wrote that her late husband had an "uncanny connection" with animals. She likened it, explained University of Florida professor Bron Taylor, "to telepathy or a sixth sense. She said Steve Irwin was able to communicate with animals and even know where they would be before other people could see or hear them."[6]

Is it possible that Irwin and other people who spend much of their time around animals are experiencing a vestige of an ancient ability to communicate with animals? If this points back to Eden, could it not also look forward to a future age when human and animals will again live peacefully together and where some form of communication is restored? Perhaps it does.

The Eschatological New Earth

Finally, do all the allusions to talking animals in myths, fairytales, and religions intimate that animals will again converse with humans in the eschatological New Earth? Is there any direct *biblical* evidence for this? Not much, but some. In Revelation 8:13, the Apostle John "heard" an eagle that was flying in midair call out in a loud voice: "Woe! Woe! Woe to the inhabitants of the earth. . ." John also writes in Revelation 5:11,13 about hearing "creatures in heaven" singing praise to God. Although Revelation was largely written in apocalyptic language, there is no reason to assume that John was not recording *literal* voices

John Wesley, as we saw in chapter eight, was a strong believer that animals will be recompensed in Heaven for the suffering they experienced from the curse and by the brutal abuses they experienced from humanity. Wesley believed that the New Earth would transcend even the Garden of Eden, and preached that all animal life will

[be] restored, not only to the vigor, strength, and swiftness which they had at their creation, but to a far higher degree of each than they ever enjoyed. They will be restored, not

only to the measure of understanding which they had in paradise, but to a degree of it as much higher than that, as the understanding of an elephant is beyond that of a worm. And whatever affections they had in the garden of God, will be restored with vast increase; being exalted and refined in a manner which we ourselves are not able to comprehend.

Later in the same sermon, Wesley added this provocative conjecture:

What, if it should then please the all-wise, the all-gracious Creator to raise them [animals] higher in the scale of beings? What, if it should please him, when he makes us "equal to angels," to make them what we are now—creatures capable of God; capable of knowing and loving and enjoying the Author of their being.[7]

Wesley is not suggesting that God will make animals equal to humans or angels in Heaven. But he is suggesting that perhaps in the New Earth animals will in some degree experience what humans presently experience on Earth today, in terms of knowing God. In other words, it may be that in the New Earth animals will be able to know, love, and enjoy God as people now do on Earth, but which, as far as we know, animals do not presently experience. Wesley did not go so far as to say that humans and animals will converse in Heaven, but certainly his comments left open the possibility that he entertained the idea.

Commenting on what animals may be like in the New Earth, Randy Alcorn poses questions worth pondering, in light of what I've shared in this chapter:

In a universe teeming with God's creativity, should talking animals or intelligent non-human beings (such as angels

and "living creatures" that not only talk but worship) surprise us? If people will be smarter and more capable on the
New Earth, should it surprise us that animals might also be
smarter and more capable?[8]

Perhaps they will.

If Animals "Talk" in the New Earth, Will It Be in a Human Language?

It's important to understand that animals in the New Earth will
still be just animals—albeit redeemed from the curse and likely
with abilities far greater than what they now possess. But they will
not possess a spiritual or moral equivalency with humans. There
is no indication in Scripture that animals in Eden were anything
other than animals, even if they were able to communicate with
Adam and Eve. We shouldn't expect it to be any different on the
New Earth.

If animals and humans are able to communicate in Heaven,
I doubt it will be through a structured, conventional language.
Communication may include some kind of verbal interchange,
but it's unlikely it will be a human-like language. Animals do not
have vocal cords and the other physical features that allow people
to speak. Communication among humans and animals in the New
Earth may be no different than the way many animal species presently communicate among themselves. Animals successfully understand each other's intentions, feelings, and desires with limited
spoken sounds—although some animals do have an amazing reper-
toire of sounds and gestures. (Crows have over 200 calls with distinct
meanings; elephants have "no fewer than 70 distinct vocalizations
with 70 distinct meanings."[9])

I believe we get a foretaste of what human/animal communication may be like in the New Earth in the relationships some people,

like Steve Irwin, have with animals. Stories abound in books and on television about horse and dog "whisperers" and other people who have a special affinity with animals—people who are able to discern their feelings and have a calming effect on aggressive or abused animals.

On the flip side, as numerous pet owners can testify, animals can frequently sense the moods, feelings, and intentions of humans. Dogs in particular—who are our oldest and closest animal companions—have little difficulty understanding human emotions, even those of strangers. Here's a personal example.

For many years my wife was a family counselor. When clients came to her office in our home, our dog Sam seemed to immediately sense the emotional state of the women my wife counseled. When they came in the front door, if they were depressed or otherwise suffering emotionally, his typical response was to lie quietly on the floor and gaze sadly into their eyes. Sometimes he would walk up to them and gently lean against their leg. This always surprised me because Sam was normally a *very* bouncy, playful dog and usually ran right up to people who came into the house. When the women left the counseling sessions, they were usually feeling better, and Sam would greet them with wagging tail and a happy look in his eyes. Sam's behavior clearly reflected his insight into the women's emotional states, and his responses were a purposeful reaction of either sympathy or joy.

To sum up, it shouldn't be surprising if the ability some people have to understand animal feelings and intentions—as well as the ability of some animals to understand these same emotions in humans—will be greatly enhanced in the New Earth to include all people and animals. Add to this the pleasure God must feel observing the devotion and care many people have for animals, and I believe we have good reason to hope He will allow the human and animal inhabitants of Heaven to communicate—in whatever way it turns out to be. After all, God "is able to do immeasurably more than all we ask or imagine" (Eph. 3:20).

Will this include some kind of *verbal* communication between humans and animals? Probably not, since animals will still be animals in Heaven without vocal cords. But will they still be able to communicate in an understandable way with God's people?

Perhaps they will.

For the Glory of God

When all is said and done, when all the evidence for animal resurrection is mustered and analyzed, if non-human creatures share the New Earth in resurrected bodies with redeemed humanity, it hinges totally on the selfless, astonishing, miraculous work of Jesus Christ. The reality of Christ's resurrection guarantees the believer's resurrection to eternal life (1Cor. 15:20-23, 49). If animals are blessed with eternal resurrected bodies, it too will depend entirely on the redeeming work of Jesus Christ for the glory of God.

At Jesus' first advent on earth, God "rescued" believers "from the dominion of darkness and brought [us] into the kingdom of the Son he loves" (Col. 1:13). Jesus reconciled "all things, whether things on earth or things in heaven, by making peace through his blood shed on the cross" (Col. 1:20). Jesus removed the fear of death (Heb. 2:14-15) and promised eternal life in Heaven for His followers (John 14:1-3).

When Jesus returns to Earth the second time, His victory over death will embrace the whole of creation. Heaven and Earth will become one, and nature's curse will be removed forever (Rev. 22:3). This heavenly New Earth will be our present Earth redeemed, renewed, and restored to its former unspoiled, uncorrupted, pristine state—as God originally created it to be. The late theologian Anthony Hoekema expressed it well:

> The work of Christ . . . is not just to save certain individuals, not even to save an innumerable throng of blood-bought people. The total work of Christ is nothing less than to redeem this entire creation from the effects of sin. That purpose will not be accomplished until God has ushered in the new earth, until Paradise Lost has become Paradise Regained.[1]

For people like me, who relish walks in the wilderness with dog companions, who are thrilled to observe nature's wild inhabitants, and who dream of the day when God's people can scratch between the ears of lions and wolves, lounge in the shadow of grizzly bears, race across meadows with deer and antelope, and perhaps even soar into the heights with eagles and hawks—such a future New Earth is indescribably exciting to anticipate. I, for one, look forward to it with eager anticipation!

APPENDIX 1

Mind Verses Brain: Scientific Evidence for Human and Animal Immortality

The mind *is that faculty of the soul that contains thoughts and beliefs along with the relevant abilities to have them.*
J. P. MORELAND, *THE SOUL*

In chapter two (and confirmed in chapter three) I demonstrated that human-like emotions, feelings, and cognition characteristic of sentient animals reflect an *immaterial* portion of their being, which is distinct from their physical brain. Thus animals, like humans, have *minds.* Since in humans, our mind is a property of our soul and survives physical death, we have every reason to believe that animals with minds also have souls that will survive physical death.

In this appendix I'll demonstrate scientifically *why* the mental activities within animal minds—just as in human minds—cannot be reduced to merely chemical and neurological brain functions. This will do two things. It gives scientific confirmation to biblical revelation that both humans and animals have souls. Second, it will corroborate the thesis of this book that humans and (at least) sentient animals can look forward to life after death in a redeemed and restored new heaven and earth.

Distinctions between Mind, Brain, and Soul

Evolutionary materialists—people who think nothing exists but physical matter and natural laws—believe that all mental activities in humans (and hence animals) can be reduced to chemical and neurological processes operating within our physical brains. They posit that all human thoughts and emotions, including religious beliefs, tastes in music, political opinions, feelings of fear, love, hate, and all other psychological states of mind, are governed (determined) by our genetic makeup as it plays out within our physical brain. There is no immaterial reality. There is no such thing as a mind distinct from the brain, let alone a soul. Thus, materialists claim that what theists (people who believe in God and an afterlife) think are non-physical (immaterial) minds or souls are merely inventions of material brains.

The most obvious consequence of this hypothesis is that what we think are free will, moral consciousness, and the ability to reason are merely illusions. Christian scholar and apologist Dinesh D'Souza describes where this philosophy leads if followed to its logical conclusion:

> If materialism is true, then no one in the world can ever refrain from anything that he or she does [because it's genetically predetermined]. The whole of morality . . . becomes an illusion.
>
> Our whole vocabulary of praise and blame, admiration and contempt, approval and disapproval would have to be eradicated. If someone murdered his neighbor, or exterminated an entire population, we would have no warrant to punish or even criticize that person because, after all, he was simply acting in the manner of a computer program malfunctioning or a stone involuntarily rolling down a hill.[1]

This materialistic hypothesis not only contradicts what we experience in the real world, in particular our understanding of emotions, free will, and moral consciousness, but it has virtually no scientific, theological, or philosophical support. In fact recent studies in brain function suggest just the opposite.[2] Its been demonstrated that human thoughts—including free will, moral consciousness, and reasoning—can *only* be explained in terms of our immaterial mind existing independent of our physical brain. This isn't hard to understand, and there are several ways to demonstrate it.

To begin with, "All, or at least most all, of the cells in the human body are regenerated or replaced every seven years."[3] Physically we are totally different persons than we were seven years ago—yet we have memories that go back to early childhood. This alone demonstrates that our mind is not identical to physical matter. Even brain cells (neurons), which apparently do not regenerate in the same fashion as other cells in our bodies, still change at a molecular level. In email correspondence with Dr. J. P. Moreland, I asked about the claim that brain cells are not replaced every seven years. His response is instructive: "The brain gains and loses atoms and molecules and they are constantly changing relationships to each other, so the brain cannot sustain personal identity over time."[4] In other words, at a sub-cellular level brain cells *do* undergo physical changes—just like all cells in the body—yet our memory and thoughts remain intact.

Here's another way to see how mind and brain are distinct features of our being. Right now you are reading this book, which contains thoughts I've generated from research and reflections on the topic of animal immortality. These thoughts are printed with ink on paper (or electronically, if you're reading a Kindle or Nook). Originally, these same thoughts were written on my computer and backed up on a USB storage device. I eventually emailed the completed manuscript to a publisher. But notice that in all these various mediums, although my thoughts remain unchanged, the printed page, computer file, and electronic transfers were all *physical* matter. If you examined this page with a magnifying glass, you would only see paper and ink. My thoughts existed in my mind *apart* from the paper and ink and *before* they were recorded in a physical form.

One more illustration may help to make this clear.

Not long ago I had the following conversation (here abridged) with a non-Christian, who is a retired lab technician in a hospital. I started the conservation by asking him this question:

"What do you think happens to you when you die?"

"You just die," he responded, "that's it."

" Then let me ask you this," I continued. "If you crack open a skull and looked inside, what would you see?"

"Your brain," he said, "you know, gray matter."

"Have you ever wondered where our thoughts come from," I pressed?

"Not really," he replied.

I then pointed out that if you put a piece of brain tissue under a microscope, you only see brain cells. What you wouldn't see are memories, feelings, and thoughts manifested in our minds. Why? Because, I explained, the mind can't be reduced to the physical proprieties of the brain. This can only mean that our mind (thoughts, memories, etc.) exists *independent* of brain matter.

"I never thought about that before," he admitted.

I went on to explain that if thoughts, emotions, and other mental activities originate in an immaterial mind that is distinct from a physical brain, it's strong evidence that our mind can exist after death. In other words, since minds aren't physical matter, they are not susceptible to physical death. And if our minds survive physical death, it can mean that people have immortal souls—since our minds are an essential property of our souls. And, I concluded, "If everyone has an immortal soul, it's vital for *you* to know where *your* soul will go after death. Eternity's a long time!"

Now, some may argue that my illustration of cracking open a skull and peering inside to see if we can observe thoughts and emotions in the brain is simplistic. I would respond by saying that the materialistic assumption that thoughts and emotions are somehow hidden in the physical tissues of brain cells is unsubstantiated reductionism. As Christian apologist and ethicist Paul Copan put it,

> It is hard to see how consciousness—human or animal—could emerge from nonconscious matter. Physical textbooks describe "matter" as having spatial extensions, shape, size, density, and so forth—but not as "being conscious." Mind and matter—though integrated—have utterly distinct properties. *Thoughts* about weight, color, shape, and size are *without* weight, color, shape, and size (emphasis Copan's).[5]

My *thoughts* about Rocky Road ice cream are not identical to the physical ingredients of Rocky Road ice cream; that is, they do not have "weight, color, shape, and size." Likewise, belief in God, taste in music, and other mental activities cannot be identified as merely physical properties of our brain. Mind and matter are entirely different properties, entirely different dimensions of our being.

Now, it is true that brains and minds work together—but they are still distinct. For example, when I hide behind a bush to observe a doe with her fawns, the light reflecting off the animals passes into my retinas, stimulates the cells in my optic nerve, which then carries data to my brain. At the same time this physical activity is going on, my *mind* is thinking how much I'd love to play with the fawns. "I wonder how soft their fur is." "I hope they survive to adulthood," and so on. In other words, as philosophy professor Chad Meister explains, "There is [a] distinction between physical events on the one hand and mental events on the other. . . . Thoughts do not seem to be the kinds of things which can be described in terms of physics, chemistry and biology. . . . Therefore, mental events and brain events are not identical; one is physical and the other is not."[6]

Neurosurgeon and professor at Harvard Medical School, Eben Alexander, provides a fascinating personal experience to illustrate this. Dr. Alexander recounts that in 2008 he contacted bacterial meningitis and lay in a coma for seven days. "Within hours," he writes, "my entire cortex—the part of the brain that controls thought and emotion and that in essence makes us human—had shut down." (This was documented by CT scans and neurological examinations.) While in this comatose state, with no brain function in his entire cortex, Dr. Alexander had what is called a "near-death experience" (NDE). In the article, Dr. Alexander shares a detailed account of this experience, which space prevents retelling. But in essence, he observed sights, sounds, and "transparent, shimmering beings." Although his experience has similarities with other accounts of NDEs, there were two profound differences.[7] He writes, "As far as I know, no one before me has ever traveled to this dimension (a) while their cortex was completely shut down, and (b) while their body was under minute medial observation, as mine was for the full seven days of my coma."[8]

Doctor Alexander's experience illustrates two facts. First, it confirms that our immaterial minds are not identical to our material (physical) brains, and second, that our immaterial minds can exist independent and outside of our physical bodies. This supports mounting scientific research that all mental states and events cannot be reduced to mere physical matter. To claim otherwise is a materialistic and philosophical assumption—not a statement of scientific fact. Dr. Alexander concludes:

Today many believe that the living spiritual truths of religion have lost their power, and that science, not faith, is the road to truth. Before my experience I strongly suspected that this was the case myself.

But I now understand that such a view is far too simple. The plain fact is that the materialist picture of the body and brain as the producers, rather than the vehicles, of human consciousness is doomed. In its place a new view of mind and body will emerge, and in fact is emerging already.[9]

More Evidence That Immaterial Minds Are Distinct from Physical Brains

Recent studies in brain science have demonstrated that changing one's thought patterns can actually *rewire* the brain. Explains British physician and medical journalist Dr. James Le Fanu: "There is abundant scientific evidence that the non-material mind can . . . directly influence the material body. . . . [J]ust *thinking about one's thoughts* physically alters the neuronal circuits of the brain" (emphasis Le Fanu's).[10] With the use of brain-imaging technology, this has been demonstrated through studies with people experiencing obsessive-compulsive disorder (OCD). Renowned research physician Jeffery Schwartz explains:

> The major scientific finding that was discovered using brain imaging was that when OCD sufferers used the power of their minds to redirect regularly their focus of attention in wholesome ways, they literally *rewired* their own brains in precisely the brain circuit that had been discovered to cause the problem. . . .
>
> Once a solid scientific theory was in place to explain how the mind's power to focus attention could systematically rewire the brain and that the language of our mental and spiritual life is necessary to empower the mind to do so, the materialist dogma was toppled. . . . [S]cience is no

longer on the side of those who claim human beings are no different in principle than a machine [i.e. philosophical materialism].[11]

This data is supported by cognitive therapy, a counseling technique used by Dr. Schwartz and other therapists. The idea is for patients to "refocus their minds away from the compulsion and . . . redirect their thoughts and actions to some activity, ideally something more pleasant. . . . [This] had the effect of re-wiring the patient's brain so that he no longer experienced the paranoid and destructive OCD urges."[12] The outcome of such therapy is changes in the way patients feel about themselves and other people.

My wife was a family counselor for many years. She used cognitive therapy techniques in her counseling ministry, teaching clients how to replace negative thought patterns (lies) with positive beliefs (truths). She can testify to many remarkable emotional healings in people who have successfully applied this kind of counseling therapy.

This is relevant to our discussion because it gives empirical confirmation that chemical and neurological processes in the brain *do not* dictate our subjective thoughts and other mental activities—just the opposite of what materialists claim. Rather, our subjective thoughts and feelings, flowing from our immaterial minds, can alter the physical functions of our brains. This is tremendously compelling evidence for the existence of immaterial souls. Why? As J. P. Moreland points out, the mind "is that faculty of the soul that contains thoughts and beliefs along with the relevant abilities to have them."[13] In short, if we have minds, we must have souls!

What about Brain Injury?

If it is true that our immaterial minds are distinct from our physical brains, why do people lose mental capabilities when their brains are injured by head trauma? Why is thinking impaired—sometimes to the point of hallucination—from alcohol or drug abuse? Along the same line, why does the mind seem to lose mental acuity as one ages? These are valid questions but not hard to explain.

It's true that head injury, substance abuse, and age can cause the brain to malfunction, and this can affect mental processes. Likewise electrical stimulation to different parts of the brain can result in various physical and mental responses. However, this only shows that while in our physical body our mind is "housed" within our brain—not that brain and mind are one and the same. As Dinesh D'Souza put it, the brain is "a kind of gateway or receiver for the mind."[14] Injury to the brain can impose certain limitations on how our thoughts are processed while our soul is confined to our physical body. But because the mind is distinct from the physical brain, injury to the brain would not obliterate the mind itself. While housed in our body, our mind may depend on a properly functioning brain to express our thoughts. But once our mind is liberated from our physical body when death occurs, it continues to exist as a faculty of our immaterial soul, fully alert and functioning.

D'Souza helps to make this clear by drawing on an essay written by American psychologist and philosopher, William James. In the essay, James explains that the physical brain is not the sole function of consciousness:

> [E]ven though our soul's life . . . may be . . . the function of a brain that perishes, yet it is not at all impossible, but on the contrary quite possible, that life may still continue when the brain itself is dead. . . . [W]hen we think . . . that thought is a function of the brain, we are not required to think of productive [i.e. causal] function only; *we are entitled also to consider permissive or transmissive function.* . . . And when finally a brain stops acting altogether or decays . . .

the sphere of being that supplied the consciousness [our mind/soul] would still be intact (emphasis James').[15]

Damage to the brain may interrupt the transmission of mental activities, but it would not affect our minds once they are disembodied from our brains, as in our souls after death. The mind itself is *not* affected by our physical condition: "When our brains die, this consciousness goes on . . . because it never died in the first place."[16] D'Souza continues: "The best evidence of contemporary neuroscience is that the mind cannot be equated with the brain, and while deterioration of the brain might impede the operation of the mind, the two are separate, which makes it possible that our immaterial minds and consciousness [i.e. our souls] might survive the termination of our physical frames."[17]

Finally, D'Souza adds this:

[C]onsciousness lies beyond all known scientific laws and explanations. The startling conclusion is that the central feature of our identity and humanity operates outside the recognized physical laws of nature. One of these laws is, of course, mortality for all living consciousness "in" the body in the same way that nerves or neurons are. Consciousness merely comes with the body and operates through the body. The body serves as a kind of receiver and transmitter for consciousness, not its author or manufacturer.[18]

Let me summarize this. While our souls reside in our physical bodies, our minds are "housed" in our brains. Thus, our brains are the vehicle through which our thoughts, feelings, and emotions are expressed—as long as our souls remain in our bodies. However, these mental activities *still* originate in our minds, not in the physical matter of brain cells. Thus, when our brains cease functioning at death, our minds continue to live on in our souls. This is compelling evidence for life after physical death.

How Does This Apply to Animals?

We saw in chapter three that sentient animals have human-like thoughts, emotions, and feelings (albeit much less sophisticated than humans). This demonstrates that they, like humans, possess immaterial minds that are distinct from their physical brains. Furthermore, because human minds are an essential property of our souls, it's legitimate to conclude that sentient animals—animals with minds—also possess souls. (Chapter four verifies that the Bible teaches animals *do have* souls, but this appendix is focusing on scientific confirmation.)

In other words, if the origin of mental activities in humans cannot be reduced to neurological and chemical processes in the brain (merely matter), and instead are associated with our immaterial minds, why would similar mental activities in animals not also originate in their immaterial minds? And to go the logical step further, if the human mind is an essential property of our soul, that part of our being which survives physical death, and if animals have minds similar to humans, it is perfectly legitimate to conclude that animals' souls also survive physical death. There is no scientific reason—or biblical—why this shouldn't be true. I like what J. P. Moreland points out:

> How do we decide what an animal's soul is like? Obviously, we cannot inspect it directly. We cannot get inside an animal's conscious life and just look at its internal states. The best approach seems to be this: Based on our direct awareness of our own inner lives, we should attribute to animals by analogy those states that are necessary to account for the animal's behavior, nothing more and nothing less.[19]

The accumulated evidence of this book—scientific, logical, and theological—leads to the highly probable conclusion that God has blessed at least sentient animals with eternal souls. In Heaven, human souls will be united with their resurrected bodies. We have every reason to believe this same wonderful future awaits soul-bearing animals.

APPENDIX 2

Harmonizing the Differences between Old and New Testament Accounts of the New Heaven and Earth

There are events and descriptions in Old Testament prophesy concerning Israel's restoration at the end of this age that appear to be contrary to the eschatological new heaven and earth revealed in Revelation. For example, people having children, growing old, and dying (Isa. 65:20, 23). On the other hand, there are also clear parallels between the two: the absence of the sun and moon (60:19; cf. Rev. 21:23; 22:5); healings of sight, deafness, and other physical disabilities (Isa. 35:5-6; cf. Rev. 21:4); everlasting joy (Isa. 35:10; cf. Rev. 21:4); a new Jerusalem and a permanent end to weeping and crying (Isa. 65:18-19; cf. Rev. 7:17; 21:2).

How should features of the new heaven and earth described differently in the Old and New Testaments be harmonized? For some interpreters, Old Testament end times prophecies[1] do not refer to the nation of Israel corporately, but to individual Jews who would be saved throughout church history. In this view, many Old Testament prophecies concerning Israel's future have a *spiritual* fulfillment in the church rather than *literal* fulfillment for the nation of Israel. This seems to be supported by Paul in Romans 2:28-29 and Galatians 6:15-16, which speak of true Jews as being followers of Christ, and by the fact that the New Testament authors considered many Old Testament prophecies to have direct application to the established church in New Testament times. If this is the case, Old Testament prophets may have had in mind a perfectly restored *earthly* kingdom under the rule of a messiah who would deliver the Jews from foreign domination, but they *unwittingly* predicted a future eternal Kingdom when the true Davidic Messiah, Jesus Christ, returns to establish the new heaven and earth in the "last days" (2 Pet. 3:10-13).

A case can also be made that Old Testament prophecies referring to a future restored Israel (e.g. Ezek. 37: 22-28) have a *dual* fulfillment—a primary and secondary application. On the one hand, they do predict a future redeemed new heaven and earth when Jesus returns to establish His eternal Kingdom. But these same prophesies refer to an *initial* Millennial Kingdom—a thousand-year reign of Jesus here on earth *prior* to the eternal heaven and earth revealed in Revelation 21:1-4. (In Revelation, the Millennial Kingdom chronologically precedes the final eschatological Heaven.)

In Romans chapter eleven, the apostle Paul writes about a future time when the covenant promises given to Israel will be fulfilled, and many Jews at that time will turn to Christ en masse (22-31). That God has a special future planed for Israel seems to be corroborated in Revelation chapter twenty-one. Here the names of the twelve tribes of Israel are written on the twelve gates of the New Jerusalem, which will descend onto the New Earth in the eschaton (see chapter five), while the names of the twelve apostles are written on the city's foundation stones. Although all believers will be part of the eternal church (the Body of Christ; Gal. 3:26-29), this suggests that in some sense the covenant promises made to Israel will be included in the eternal Kingdom. This is best explained in the Millennial Kingdom view.

During the Millennial Kingdom, God will bring about a *literal* fulfillment of all the Old Testament promises of a restored Israel. Satan will be imprisoned and the world will enjoy an unparalleled period of joy and prosperity under Christ's rule. After this thousand-year period, Satan will be released for a short time to spearhead a final rebellion against God, after which he and his underlings, along with unsaved humans, will be cast into the Lake of Fire (hell) forever (see Rev. 20:1-10). At that point, Heaven and the redeemed and restored Earth will be *united* to become the New Earth (see chapter five), and all believers will enjoy eternal bliss with our Lord Jesus Christ (21:1).

In either view, what is important to understand is that Old Testament prophecies—like their New Testament counterparts—clearly describe a Kingdom with characteristics unlike anything imaginable on Earth today. In particular, the prophesied Jewish Messiah who will usher in the restoration of Israel in the Millennial Kingdom scenario is clearly more than just human. Among His other traits, Daniel speaks of Him as having "authority, glory and sovereign power," being "worshiped" by all people, and having a kingdom "that will never end." Only Jesus fulfills the prophecies of this future Messiah (Dan. 7:13-14; also Isa. 9:6-7).

My point is neither theological stance contradicts the *facts* and *features* of an eschatological new heaven and earth. But again, it does seem that the least complicated end-times scenario, in terms of harmonizing the differences between Old Testament prophecies of a restored Israel with Revelation, would be the Millennial Kingdom view. It will fulfill God's promises to restore Israel as well as show that the true Messiah, Jesus Christ, will fulfill His prophesied role of sitting on the throne of David as the eternal ruler of redeemed Israel (see Luke 1:30-33). Moreover, without this perspective, the huge amount of details given in Old Testament prophecies concerning the anticipated Davidic kingdom would be reduced to merely figurative language and symbolism—spiritualizing what clearly reads as predictive history. It's hard to imagine that God would give so much information and description of restored Israel if it did not have a literal fulfillment.

Whether or not there will be a literal Millennial Kingdom does not change the fact that the Jewish prophetic vision of a new heaven and earth, and the New Testament fulfillment of Heaven united with Earth (the New Earth), is speaking of the same redeemed, glorious eternal Kingdom of God: Heaven. Heaven will encompass the restored New Earth, and God will dwell there with His people. All resurrected believers will live forever in Heaven *on* New Earth.

About the Author

Dan Story has made good use of his BA in theology and his MA in Christian apologetics. He's taught college classes, led Bible studies, and spearheaded seminars. He's also authored a variety of books and articles on everything from the defense of the Christian faith to the environment.

Dan's media presence isn't limited to his published works. He's been a guest on more than sixty-five radio programs, and he's even appeared on television.

The father of two and grandfather of four, Dan is married and lives in Southern California. Apart from writing and teaching, Dan enjoys mountain biking, hiking, reading, and photographing wildlife. Learn more about Dan's life and work at www.danstory.net.

ENDNOTES

Introduction

1. See http://abcnews.go.com/sections/us/DailyNews/pets_beliefnetpoll010720.html.
2. Note of clarification. In the Bible Heaven is not capitalized. However, throughout this book I will capitalize Heaven when I'm referring to God's dwelling place and to the future "united" heaven and Earth; that is, where God will dwell with His people as described in Revelation 21:1- 2 (see chapter five). I'll leave heaven lowercase when it refers to Earth's atmosphere and visible outer space. When I use "new heaven and earth," I'm using it in the same prophetic sense it's used in Scripture, therefore, as in the Bible, the phrase will be in lowercase. Finally, I'll use "New Earth" when specifically emphasizing the restored and redeemed planet Earth in the eschaton.
3. San Diego Union-Tribune, 9-1-89, comic section.
4. C. S. Lewis, *The Problem of Pain* (New York: Macmillan Publishing Co., Inc., 1962), 137.

Chapter 1

1. Camilo Mora, Derek P. Tittensor, Sina Adl, Alastair G. B. Simpson, and Boris Worm, "How many Species Are There on Earth and in the Oceans," *A Peer-Review Journal,* August 2011. http://www.plosbiology.org/article/info%3Adoi%2F10.1371%2Fjournal.pbio.1001127.
2. Dan Story, *Should Christians Be Environmentalists?* (Grand Rapids: Kregel Publications, 2012), Chapter 8.
3. Susan P. Bratton, *Christianity, Wilderness and Wildlife: The Original Desert Solitaire* (London: University of Scranton Press, 2009), 292.
4. In 1 Corinthians 9:9-10, Paul appears to reinterpret the intent of Deuteronomy 25:4. However, Paul is merely drawing an additional application from this passage by giving a spiritual (and practical)

principle: If we allow domesticated animals to benefit from their labor, even more so should the apostles, who are laboring for the Gospel, be supported by the church. Paul is not contradicting what is a clear instruction in Deuteronomy, nor is he suggesting that God does not care about the oxen feeding while threshing grain. It is not unusual for New Testament writers to grasp and apply additional insights from Old Testament Scriptures.

5. Bratton, *Christianity, Wilderness and Wildlife*, 298.
6. Richard Bauckham, *Living With Other Creatures: Green Exegesis and Theology* (Waco, TX: Baylor University Press, 2011), 222.
7. Peter Singer, *Animal Liberation: A New Ethics for Our Treatment of Animal* (New York: A New York Review Book, distributed by Random House, Inc., 1975), 209.

Chapter 2

1. Angela Hunt, *Unspoken* (Nashville: WestBow Press, 2005), 11.
2. Taken from Descartes' 1646 letter to the Marquess of Newcastle, http://pubpages.unh.edu/~jel/Descartes.html
3. Jeffrey Kluger, *The Animal Mind* (New York: Time Books, 2014), 4. This book is an excellent introductory survey of recent discoveries in animal behavior. It includes numerous examples along with beautiful photographs.
4. Marc Bekoff, *Animal Passions and Beastly Virtues* (Philadelphia: Temple University Press, 2006), 15, 28.
5. Carl Safina, *Beyond Words: What Animals Think and Feel* (New York: Henry Holt and Company, LLC, 2015), 395.
6. Marc Bekoff, *The Emotional Lives of Animals: A Leading Scientist Explores Animal Joy, Sorrow, and Empathy—and Why They Matter* (Novato, CA: New World Library, 2007), 46-47.
7. Bekoff, *Animal Passions and Beastly Virtues*, 25-27.
8. Richard Bauckham, *The Bible and Ecology: Rediscovering the Community of Creation* (Waco, TX: Baylor University Press, 2010), 53.

9. J. I. Packer, *Knowing God* (Downers Grove: InterVarsity Press, 1973), 153.

10. Konrad Z. Lorena, *King Solomon's Ring: New Light on Animal Ways* (New York: Thomas Y. Crowell Company, 1970), 147.

11. American Veterinary Medical Associations, "U. S. Pet Ownership Statistics," p. 1
https://www.avma.org/KB/Resources/Statistics/Pages/Market- research-statistics- US-pet-ownership.aspx.

12. Marc Bekoff, *The Emotional Lives of Animals*, xx, 10.

Chapter 3

1. John Steinbeck, *Travels with Charley* (New York: The Viking Press, Inc., 1962), 146-147.

2. I am not a trained ethologist (a scientist who studies animal behavior), so in this chapter I will refer to and quote several of the best authorities on animal behavior.

3. Dean Koontz, *A Big Little Life: A Memoir of a Joyful Dog* (New York: Hyperion, 2009), 81.

4. Mark Bekoff, *The Emotional Lives of Animals: A Leading Scientist Explores Animal Joy, Sorrow, and Empathy—and Why They Matter* (Novato, CA: New World Library, 2007), 45.

5. Richard Gray, "Animals can tell right from wrong," *The Telegraph*, May 23, 2009. See http://www.telegraph.co.uk/earth/wildlife/5373379/Animals- can-tell-right-from-wrong.html.

6. Bekoff, *The Emotional Lives of Animals*, xix.

7. Jennifer S. Holland, *Unlikely Friendships: 47 Remarkable Stories from the Animal Kingdom* (New York: Workman Publishing, 2011).

8. "Dolphins save dog," The San Diego Union-Tribune, 3-14-11, E-3.

9. Carl Safina, *Beyond Words; What Animals Think and Feel* (New York: Henry Holt and Company, 2015), 371.

10. Bekoff, *The Emotional Lives of Animals,* 17.

11. Ibid., 16.

12. Safina, *Beyond Words,* 352-355.

13. Mike MacIntosh, *When Your World Falls Apart: Life Lessons From A Ground Zero Chaplin* (Colorado Springs: Victor, 2002), 91-93.

14. Bekoff, *The Emotional Lives of Animals,* 63.

15. Ibid., 66.

16. Mark Bekoff, *Animal Passions and Beastly Virtues* (Philadelphia: Temple University Press, 2006), 15.

17. Safina, *Beyond Words,* 73.

18. Jeffrey Kluger, *The Animal Mind* (New York: Time Books, 2014), 53.

19. Bekoff, *The Emotional Lives of Animals,* 3.

20. Kluger, *The Animal Mind,* 18.

21. Konrad Z. Lorenz, *King Solomon's Ring: New Light on Animal Ways* (New York: Thomas Y. Crowell Company, 1970), 79.

22. Benedict Carey, "Researchers' study finds that mice are capable of showing empathy," Science Section, The San Diego Union-Tribune, July 13, 2006, E-3.

23. Bekoff, *Animal Passions and Beastly Virtues,* Part Three.

24. Jeffrey Kluger, *The Animal Mind,* 78.

25. Bekoff, *The Emotional Lives of Animals,* 54.

26. Ted Kerasote, *Merle's Door: Lessons from a Freethinking Dog* (Orlando: Harcourt, Inc., 2007), 243,311.

27. Safina, *Beyond Words,* 238.

28. Glen Martin, *Game Changer: Animals Rights and the Fate of Africa's Wildlife* (Berkeley: University of California Press, 2012), 170.

29. Karl von Frisch, *Animal Architecture,* translated by Lisbeth Gombrich (New York: Harcourt Brace Jovanovich, 1974).

30. Craig Childs, *The Animal Dialogues: Uncommon Encounters in the Wild* (New York: Back Bay Books, Little, Brown and Company, 2009), 129.

31. Natalie Angier, "Animal World's Best Toolmakers are Proud Parents, too", San Diego Union-Tribune, 2-21-11, E-3.

32. "Scratching an Itch," San Diego Union-Tribune, Science and Environment section, 3-12-12, A3.

33. Kerasote, *Merle's Door*, 245.

34. Safina, *Beyond Words*, 43, 51.

35. Lorenz, *King Solomon's Ring*, 144-145.

36. Ibid., 82-83.

37. Bekoff, *The Emotional Lives of Animals*, 14.

38. Kluger, *The Animal Mind*, 104.

39. Alexandra Horowitz, *Inside of a Dog: What Dogs See, Smell, and Know* (New York: Scribner, 2009), 225, 228.

40. Bekoff, *Animal Passions and Beastly Virtues*, 13.

41. Safina, *Beyond Words*, 79.

42. Holland, *Unlikely Friendships*, 193.

43. C. S. Lewis, *The problem of Pain* (New York: MacMillian Publishing Co., Inc.:1962), 138.

44. "Self-awareness," EARTH WATCH, The San Diego Union-Tribune, 10-2010, E-3.

45. Horowitz, *Inside of a Dog*, 220.

46. Bekoff, *Animal Passions and Beastly Virtues*, 69.

47. Safina, *Beyond Words*, 278.

48. Martin, *Game Changer*, 91.

Chapter 4

1. James Herriot, *James Herriot's Favorite Dog Stories* (New York: St. Martin's Press, 1995), 30-32.

2. J. P. Moreland, "Does the Bible Teach That Humans Are More Than Their Bodies?" in *The Apologetics Study Bible* (Nashville: Holman Bible Publishers, 2007), 1895.

3. Gary R. Habermas and J.P. Moreland, *Immortality: The Other Side of Death* (Nashville: Thomas Nelson Publishers, 1992), 51.

4. Stephen M. Vantassel, *Dominion over Wildlife? An Environmental Theology of Human-Wildlife Relations* (Eugene, OR: Resource Publications, 2009), 33 cf. 177.
5. Paul Badham, "Do Animals have Immortal Souls?" In *Animals on the Agenda: Questions about Animals for Theology and Ethics*, ed. Andrew Linzey and Dorothy Yamamoto (Chicago: University of Illinois Press, 1998), p. 181-182.
6. Habermas and Moreland, *Immortality*, p. 51.
7. Walter A. Elwell, ed., Evangelical *Dictionary of Theology* (Grand Rapids: Baker Books, 1997), p. *1036*.
8. Spiros Zodhiates, *The Complete Word Study Dictionary New Testament* (Chattanooga, TN: AMG Publishers, 1993),1180.
9. Steve W. Lemke, "Does the Bible Affirm That Animals Have Rights?" in *The Apologetic Study Bible*, 298.
10. The following passages are from the New American Standard Bible.
11. The following passages are from the New American Standard Bible.
12. Randy Alcorn, *Heaven* (Carol Stream, IL: Tyndale House Publishers, Inc., 2004), 385.
13. See Dan Story, *Should Christians Be Environmentalists?* (Grand Rapids: Kregel Publications, 2012).
14. Ibid., chapter 5.
15. Andrew Linzey, Introduction to Part Three, "Disputed Questions," *Animals on the Agenda*, Linzey and Yamamoto, eds., p. 119.

Chapter 5

1. Dean Ohlman, "Animals in the Peaceable Kingdom," http://restoringeden.org/resources/Ohlman/AnimalsPeacableKingdom.
2. Walter A. Elwell, ed., Evangelical *Dictionary of Theology* (Grand Rapids: Baker Books, 1084), 763.

3. Hank Hanegraaff, *Afterlife: What You Need to Know About Heaven, the Hereafter & Near-Death Experiences* (Brentwood, TN: Worthy Publishing, 2013), 20, 132.
4. M. Daniel Carroll R. "A Biblical Theology of the City and the Environment: Human Community in the Created Order," in *Keeping God's Earth*, ed. Noah J. Toly & Daniel I. Block (Downers Grove: IVP Academic, 2010), 86.
5. Anthony A. Hoekema, "Heaven: Not Just an Eternal Day Off," *Christianity Today* (June 6, 2003), Http://www.christianitytoday. com/ct/channel/utilities/print.html?id=7414.
6. This argument is fallacious for reasons other than my response here. In my book S*hould Christians Be Environmentalists?* I present a thorough theological and apologetic assessment of the Bible's overall perspective on environmental stewardship and ethics. See Dan Story, *Should Christians Be Environmentalists?* (Grand Rapids: Kregel Publications, 2012).
7. Spiros Zodhiates, *The Complete Word Study Dictionary: New Testament* (Chattanooga, TN: AMG Publishers, 1993), 804.
8. Douglas J. Moo, "Eschatology and Environmental Ethics: On the importance of Biblical Theology to Creation Care," *Keeping God's Earth: Global Environment in Biblical Perspective*, ed. Noah J. Toly and Daniel I. Block (Downers Grove: IVP Academic, 2010), 34-35.
9. Steven Bouma – Prediger, *For the Beauty of the Earth: A Christian Vision for Creation Care*, 2nd ed. (Grand Rapids: Baker Academic, 2010), 68-69.
10. Susan E. Schreiner, *The Theater of His Glory: Nature and the Natural Order in the Thought of John Calvin* (Grand Rapids: Baker Books, 1991), 97-99.

Chapter 6

1. Randy Alcorn, *Safely Home* (Wheaton: Tyndale House Publishers, 2001), 376.

2. Richard Bauckham, *The Bible and Ecology: Rediscovering the Community of Creation* (Waco, TX: Baylor University Press), 103-105.
3. Ibid., 124.
4. Randy Alcorn, *Heaven* (Carol Stream IL: Tyndale House Publishers, inc., 2004), 158, 377, 378.
5. C. S. Lewis, *The Weight of Glory* (San Francisco: HarperSanFrancisco, 1980), 29-33.
6. Wallace Stegner, *Wolf Willow, A History, a Story, and a Memory of the Last Plains Frontier* (New York: Ballantine Books, 1962), 19.
7. C. S. Lewis, *Mere Christianity* (New York: Macmillan Publishing, 1952), 120.
8. Arthur O. Roberts, *Exploring Heaven: What Great Christian Thinkers Tell Us About Our Afterlife with God* (San Francisco: HarperSanFrancisco), 2003, 66.
9. Alister McGrath, *The Reenchantment of Nature: The Denial of Religion and the Ecological Crisis* (New York: Doubleday / Galilee, 2003), 184-183.
10. Alister E. McGrath, *A Brief History of Heaven* (Malden, MA: Blackwell Publishing, 2003), 78.
11. McGrath, *The Reenchantment of Nature*, 24, 141.
12. Alister McGrath, *Glimpsing the Face of God: The Search for Meaning in the Universe* (Grand Rapids: William B. Eerdmans Publishing Company, 2002), 9, 13, 112.

Chapter 7

1. H. Paul Santmire, *Brother Earth: Nature, God, and Ecology in Time of Crisis* (New York: Thomas Nelson, 1970), 109-110.
2. WebBible encyclopedia. http://www.christiananswers.net/dictionary/animals.html.
3. Peter Kreeft, *Every Thing You Ever Wanted to Know about Heaven . . . But Never Dreamed of Asking* (San Francisco: Ignatius Press,1990), 45-46.

4. Richard Bauckham, *Living With Other Creatures: Green Exegesis and Theology* (Waco TX: Baylor University Press, 2011), 75.
5. Ibid.
6. Ibid., 76.
7. Richard Bauckham, "Jesus and Animals II: What did he Practise?" [sic], in *Animals on the Agenda: Questions about Animals for Theology and Ethics*, eds. Andrew Linzey & Dorothy Yamamoto (Chicago: University of Illinois Press, 1998), 58.
8. Bauckham, *Living With Other Creatures*, 76.
9. Ibid., 119.
10. Ibid., 130.
11. Richard Bauckham, *The Bible and Ecology: Rediscovering the Community of Creation* (Waco, TX: Baylor University Press, 2010), 79.
12. Bauckham, *Living With Other Creatures*, 177,165 respectively.
13. Ibid., 178.
14. Ibid., 149.
15. Randy Alcorn, *Heaven* (Carol Stream IL: Tyndale House Publishers, Inc., 2004), 379-380.
16. Daniel I. Block, "To Serve and to Keep," in *Keeping God's Earth: The Global Environment in Biblical Perspective*, ed. Noah J. Toly and Daniel I. Block (Downers Grove: IVP Academic, 2010), 121.

Chapter 8

1. Arthur O. Roberts, *Exploring Heaven: What Great Christian Thinkers Tell Us About Our Afterlife with God* (San Francisco: HarperSanFrancisco), 96.
2. Since humans and animals were vegetarians, the dominion instructions God gave Adam in Genesis 1:26 (and subsequently the entire human race) would not have included killing animals. Rather, dominion as God intended it would have included companionship, instrumental use, and stewardship

responsibilities over animals. It would have precluded abuse, harmful exploitation, and confinement. These practices would have been nonexistent and unnecessary in God's original design for human/animal relationships. See my book *Should Christians Be Environmentalists?* (Grand Rapids: Kregel Publications, 2012), chapter eight.

3. Hanlee H. Barnette, *The Church and the Ecological Crisis* (Grand Rapids: Eerdmans, 1972), 40.

4. John Calvin, *Commentary on the Epistle of Paul to the Romans*, trans. John Owen (1849). Quoted in Michael J. Murray, *Nature Red in Tooth & Claw: Theism and the Problem of Animal Suffering* (Oxford: Oxford University Press), 79.

5. David Clough, "The Anxiety of the Human Animal: Martin Luther on Non-human Animals and Human Animality," in *Creaturely Theology: On God, Humans and Other Animals*, Ed. Celia Deane-Drummond and David Clough (London: SCM Press, 2009), 41-60. Quoted in htttp://chesterrep.openrespository.com/cdr/bitstream/10034/133992/1/1-2%20Chapter%202%20DC%20%20-%20%20A.pdf, 2.

6. "General Deliverance, Sermon 60," a message preached by John Wesley, November 30, 1781. With comments and summaries by Randy Alcorn, Eternal Perspective Ministries. http://www.epm.org/resourcess/2010/Feb/21/general-deliverance-sermon-60/, 3.

7. See "Will Animals be Redeemed," Petroc and Eldred Wiley, in *Animals on the Agenda: Questions about Animals for Theology and Ethics*, eds. Andrew Linzey & Dorothy Yamamoto (Chicago: University of Illinoise Press, 1909), chapter 16.

8. H. Paul Santmire, *Brother Earth: Nature, God, and Ecology in Time of Crisis* (New York: Thomas Nelson, 1970), 163.

9. Randy Alcorn, *Heaven* (Tyndale House Publishing, Inc.; © Eternal Perspective Ministries, 2004), 386.

10. Michael J. Murray, *Nature Red in Tooth & Claw*, 122.

11. Andrew Linzey, "Introduction" [to Part Three], *Animals on the Agenda*, 118.
12. C. S. Lewis, *The Problem of Pain*, (New York: Macmillan Publishers, 1962), 137-38.
13. J. P. Moreland, *The Soul: How We Know It's Real and Why It Matters* (Chicago: Moody Publishers, 2014), 142.

Chapter 9

1. Arden Dier, "Pope Francis says dogs can go to heaven," in http://www.usatoday.com/story/news/nation-now/2014/12/12/pope-francis-dogs-can-go-to-heaven/20296955/.
2. David Gibson, "Sorry, Fido. Pope Francis didn't say pets go to heaven," in http://www.usatoday.com/story/news/world/2014/12/13/pope-francis-animals-heaven-debunked/20352275/.
3. Andrew Linzey, "Introduction" [to Part Two], in *Animals on the Agenda: Questions about Animals for Theology and Ethics*, eds. Andrew Linzey & Dorothy Yamamoto (Chicago: University of Illinois Press, 1909), 65.
4. Quoted in Scott Ickert, "Luther and Animals: Subject to Adam's Fall," in *Animals on the Agenda*, 91.
5. David Clough, "The Anxiety of the Human Animal: Martin Luther on Non-human Animals and Human Animality," in *Creaturely Theology: On God, Humans and Other Animals*, Ed. Celia Deane-Drummond and David Clough. (London: SCM Press, 2009), 41-60. Quoted in htttp://chesterrep.openrespository.com/cdr/bitstream/10034/133992/1/1-2%20Chapter%202%20DC%20%20-%20%20A.pdf, 13.
6. Michael J. Murray, *Nature Red in Tooth & Claw: Theism and the Problem of Animal Suffering* (Oxford: Oxford University Press), 124.
7. Quoted in Nekeisha Alexis-Baker and John Rempel, "Theology for the Dogs: Why Nonhuman Animals Matter to Creation," http://

www.jesusradicals.com/wp-content/uploads/theologyfordogs. pdf, 9.

8. Ibid., 9-10.

9. John Calvin, *Commentaries on the Epistle of Paul the Apostle to the Romans*, trans. John Owen (Grand Rapids: Christian Classics Ethereal Library), http://www.ccel.org/ccel/calvin/calcom38. all.html#xii.

10. Quoted in Susan E. Schreiner, *The Theater of His Glory; Nature & the Natural Order in the Thoughts of John Calvin* (Grand Rapids: Baker Books, 1991), 98.

11. Murray, *Nature Red in Tooth & Claw*, 123.

12. Jay B. McDaniel, "Can Animal Suffering be Reconciled with Belief in an All-Loving God," in *Animals on the Agenda*, 169.

13. "General Deliverance Sermon 60," 3.

14. "Animals Matter to God: Animals in Theology, Ethics, History & Law: A Review, June 16, 2012 in http://animalsmattertogod. com/tag/bishop-joseph-butler-and- animal-resurrection/

15. Quoted in *Lectures on Butler's Analog of Religion, to the Constitution and the Course of Nature*, Lecture II, "A Future Life, 24-25. https:// books.google.com/books?id=6zS11eiTfMAC&pg=PA25&lpg= PA25&dq=joseph+butler+and+animal+resurrection&source= bl&ots=JDBpyvx_3m&sig=ZTAlvoruFlnyV6lVQR1v4_n6V48& hl=en&sa=X&ei=tXaQVJCWEcSkNv-HgpAD&ved= 0CDcQ6AEwBg#v=onepage&q=joseph%20butler%20and%20 animal%20resurrection&f=false.

16. Peter Kreeft, *Everything You Ever Wanted to Know about Heaven . . . But Never Dreamed of Asking* (San Francisco: Ignatius Press, 1990), 45-46.

17. Hank Hanegraaff, *Resurrection* (Nashville: Thomas Nelson, Inc.), 120-122.

18. Randy Alcorn, *Heaven* (Carol Stream, IL Tyndale House Publishing, Inc., 2004), 386.

19. Dan Story, "Rethinking the Biblical Perspective on Ecology," *Christian Research Journal*, Vol. 35 / No. 03 (May/June) 2012, 58-59, 63.

20. Richard Bauckham, *The Bible and Ecology: Rediscovering the Community of Creation* (Waco, TX: Baylor University Press, 2010), 171.

21. Quoted from email correspondence, December 15, 2011.

22. C. S. Lewis, *The Problem of Pain* (New York: Macmillan Publishers, 1962), 137.

23. Ibid.

24. Ibid., 138.

25. Ibid.

26. Ibid., 139.

27. Ibid., 141.

Chapter 10

1. Angela Hunt, *Unspoken* (Nashville, TN: WestBow Press, 2005), 172-73.

2. Randy Alcorn, *Heaven* (Carol Stream, IL: Tyndale House Publishers, 2004), 390.

3. I give suggestions on how to find and observe wildlife without frightening them away in my book, *Where Wild Things Live: Wildlife Watching Techniques and Adventures* (Happy Camp, CA: Naturegraph Publishers, 2009).

4. Rick Weiss, "Without Predators, Prey Fear Wanes," The San Diego Union/Tribune, 7-5-07, p. D-1.

5. Jeffrey Kluger, *The Animal Mind* (New York: Time Books, 2014), 77.

6. Bron Taylor, *Dark Green Religion: Nature Spirituality and the Planetary Future* (Berkeley, CA: University of California Press, 2010), 146.

7. The "General Deliverance, Sermon 60." http://www.whdl.org/content/general-deliverance-sermon-60.-

8. Randy Alcorn, *Heaven*, 390.

9. Jeffrey Kluger, *The Animal Mind*, 67.

For the Glory of God

1. Quoted in Randy Alcorn, *Heaven* (Carol Stream, IL: Tyndale House Publishers, 2004), 104.

Appendix 1

1. Dinesh D'Souza, *What's So Great About Christianity* (Carol Stream, IL: Tyndale House Publishers, 2008), 252-253.

2. See, James Le Fanu, *Why Us? How Science Rediscovered the Mystery of Ourselves* (London: HarperPress, 2009); Dinesh D'Souza, *Live After Death: The Evidence* (Washington DC: Regnery Publishing, Inc., 2009), ch. 7 & 8.

3. Chad V. Meister, "A PHILOSOPHICAL AND HISTORICAL CASE FOR LIFE AFTER DEATH, "Areopagus *Journal,* Fall 2011, 16.

4. Email correspondence with J. P. Moreland, 4-16-2012.

5. Paul Copan, "Does Religion Originate in the Brains?" *Christian Research Journal,* Vol. 31, No. 02, 37-38.

6. Meister, *Areopagus Journal,* 15

7. Although near death experiences are compelling evidence for life after death, people who experience them give different accounts of what they observe—and often the accounts differ from the data Scriptures reveals about the afterlife. Therefore, we should not assume NDEs to give accurate descriptions of Heaven.

8. Eben Alexander, "Heaven Is Real: A Doctor's Experience of the Afterlife," http://www.newsweek.com/proof-heaven-doctors-experience-afterlife-65327.

9. Ibid.

10. Le Fanu, *Why Us?,* 219, 220.

11. Jeffrey Schwartz, "Mind Transcending Matter," *World*, April 3, 2004, 43, 45.

12. Dinesh D'Souza, *Life After Death: The Evidence* (Washington DC: Regnery Publishing, Inc., 2009),130.

13. Moreland, *The Soul: How We Know It's Real and Why It Matters* (Chicago: Moody Publisher, 2014). 140-141.

14. D'Souza, *Life After Death*, 113.

15. William James, "Human Immortality (1898)": http://www.uky.edu/~eushe2/Pajares/jimmortal.html.

16. D'Souza, *Life After Death*, 114.

17. Dinesh D'Souza, *Life After Death*,125.

18. Ibid.,136.

19. Moreland, *The Soul*, 141-142.

Appendix 2

1. See Isaiah 35:1-10; 65:17-25; Joel 3:18-21.

CPSIA information can be obtained
at www.ICGtesting.com
Printed in the USA
LVOW04s1027301016
510896LV00009B/578/P